M000107023

BEST BOOKSTORES
IN CALIFORNIA AND THE WEST

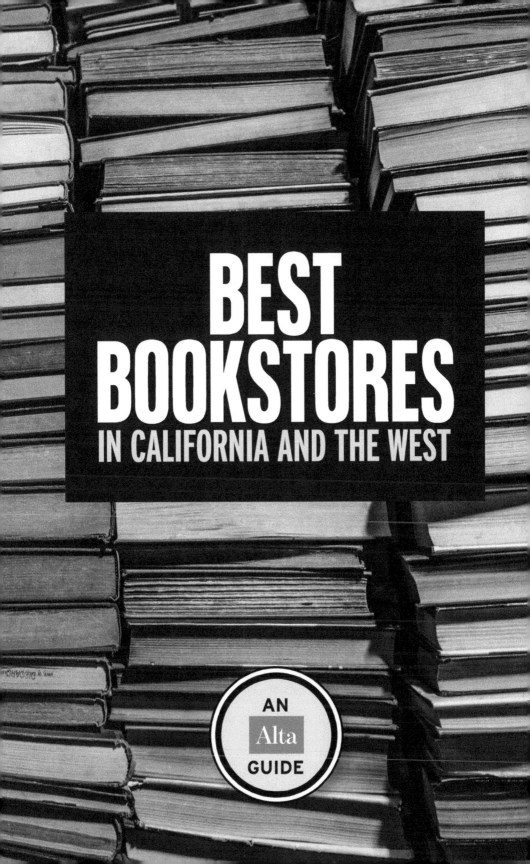

BEST BOOKSTORES
IN CALIFORNIA AND THE WEST

AN
Alta
GUIDE

© 2023 *Alta Journal*

All rights reserved. This book or any portion
thereof may not be reproduced or used in any
manner whatsoever without the express written
permission of the publisher except for the use of
brief quotations in a book review.

Alta Journal
P.O. Box 14666
San Francisco, CA 94114
altaonline.com

Print ISBN: 978-1-7350758-5-3

TABLE OF CONTENTS

Book Soup, page 27

Downtown Book & Sound, page 51

Builders Booksource, page 76

Powell's Books, page 100

City Lights
Booksellers and
Publishers in San
Francisco's North
Beach neighborhood.

Our Cultural Centers

The once and future bookstores
of California and the West beckon us.

hat is a bookstore if not a community? I've been consid-
ering such a question for most of my life. I was raised in
bookstores, or at least around them; from the age of 9 or
10, they have been my favorite haunts. I can remember,
as a middle schooler, mapping out walks across Manhat-
tan (where I was born and raised) around the bookstores I intended to check
out. There were dozens of them in those days, and the routine was always similar: Step inside and, first, feel the overwhelming possibility of all those titles,
with all their stories. Then take a deep breath and, starting with the new releases, work my way through the shelves and tables piled with books.

The routine didn't change after I began to work in bookstores or when I
left New York. In Europe, I spent the summer after college visiting so many
bookshops in so many countries that I had to buy a suitcase to get my purchases home. On the West Coast—the Bay Area and later Southern California—I
sought out bookstores as if they were holy sites: Moe's and Cody's in Berkeley,
Dutton's Brentwood and Book Soup in West Hollywood. A particular touch-
stone was North Beach's City Lights, which turns 70 this year. Other than
(perhaps) the Gotham Book Mart and the original Shakespeare and Company
on the Left Bank, has there ever been a bookstore as important to me?

I remember the first time I saw it; I was 18 and newly arrived in San Francisco. This was 1980, and I made the pilgrimage on foot, wandering from my
studio in the Haight to Market Street, turning toward Chinatown and North
Beach. I was struck by what felt to me to be the inevitability of the place, the
banner—"CITY LIGHTS Booksellers & Publishers," it declared—staking a
claim to that stretch of Columbus Avenue, the black-and-white checkerboard
flooring in the central room. I understood the history, knew the shop had expanded from a tiny storefront, now the vestibule that housed the cash register
and assorted memorabilia. I recalled the famous photo, taken in 1956, just
three years after City Lights opened, of Neal Cassady, Allen Ginsberg, and

City Lights has served as a literary meeting place since 1953.

PENNI GLADSTONE

Lawrence Ferlinghetti, along with some others, standing in front of the store. The image was so crisp, so alluring (to me, at least), that it felt almost as if, were I to squint my eyes in just the right way, I might somehow manage to step inside the frame.

Ferlinghetti would later tell me he had been inspired by what he'd seen in Europe. "I'd been in France on the G.I. Bill," he recollected. "And it seemed that the big bookstores in France—Gallimard and Hachette—were publishers also. That was where the original idea came from." He'd also observe that "from the beginning, the aim was to publish across the board, avoiding the provincial and the academic, and not publishing (that pitfall of the small press) just 'our gang.' I had in mind rather an international, dissident, insurgent ferment." I loved that idea then, and I still do: the notion that a bookstore can be a cultural center, but even more that the culture it represents can (must) always be outward looking instead of insular. This, too, is what I've long loved about bookshops, that they are expansive. They exist to challenge our beliefs rather than to reaffirm them. They exist not only to connect us but also in some fundamental sense to introduce, or reintroduce, us to the world.

Over the years, I've fallen in love with everything about City Lights, from the odd books in the basement to the publishing offices upstairs. My favorite corners include the poetry room, where I've read on more than one occasion, and the back stairwell, with its self-published and DIY chapbooks and zines. This, too, is what a bookstore should stand for, this (yes) *insurgent ferment*, the community speaking for itself. It's a defining ethos of City Lights: the range, the scope, the willingness to showcase as much of everything as it can offer, to present voices from across the board.

In that sense, City Lights is, to me, a kind of model, an exemplar of how a bookstore ought to run. Something similar, I think, might be said of a new venue, the North Figueroa Bookshop, in the Los Angeles neighborhood of

The North Figueroa Bookshop, founded in 2023, caters to the needs of Los Angeles's Highland Park neighborhood.

CHRISTINA GANDOLFO

Highland Park. I visited last summer before it opened. There were no books yet, but that was fine: those empty shelves spoke to me of another sort of possibility. Decades ago, I was on the staff that opened an independent bookstore in Lower Manhattan; I can still remember stocking its shelves as if I were participating in a spiritual ritual. Spiritual indeed, a kind of cleansing, each new title signifying and embracing our deliriously provocative humanity. Like City Lights, the North Figueroa Bookshop is linked to a publisher—more than one of them, in fact. It shares space with two Los Angeles independents, Unnamed Press and Rare Bird, with additional financing from New York publishers Grove Atlantic and Farrar, Straus and Giroux/MCD Books.

Do I need to say how happy this makes me? Do I need to say that this is a necessary mission, a spiritual ritual of its own? Not long ago, after all, Highland Park lost another bookstore, the gloriously idiosyncratic Book Show. In that sense, North Figueroa is performing community service at a crucial level, bringing a bookshop back to the neighborhood. At the same time, there is that consortium model, which brings publishers to bookselling in a way that feels both innovative and traditional at once. Those bookstores I once frequented in Manhattan? Many had publishing roots. Scribner's, Doubleday...it wasn't just Europe or San Francisco, in other words. It used to be an infrastructural commonplace. And why not?

If a bookstore is a community, so too is all of literary culture, a landscape of discovery at its most profound. What better mechanism, then, to surprise or ennoble us than going back to the future, rethinking the bookstore in its most essential form? ■

—David L. Ulin

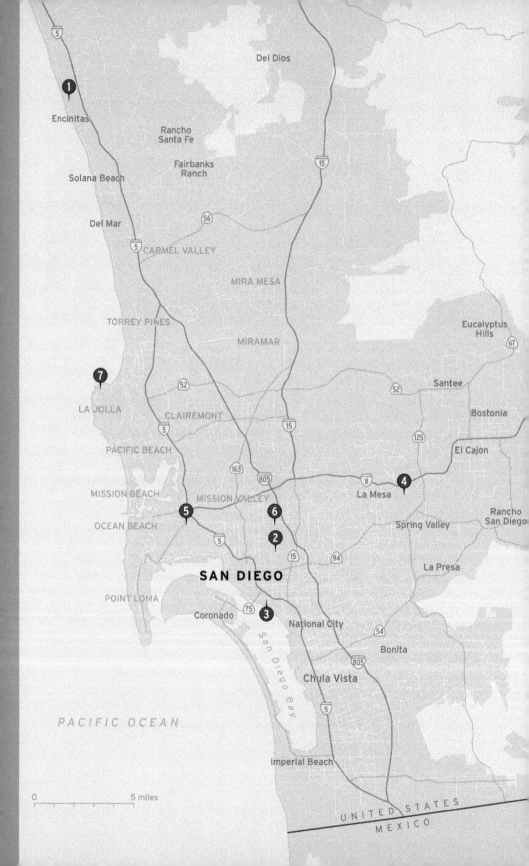

BOOKSTORES | LEGEND

1 ARTIFACT BOOKS
603 S. Coast Hwy. 101, Encinitas

2 THE BOOK CATAPULT
3010B Juniper St., San Diego

3 LIBÉLULA
950 S. 26th St., San Diego

4 MAXWELL'S HOUSE OF BOOKS
8285 La Mesa Blvd., La Mesa

5 MYSTERIOUS GALAXY
3555 Rosecrans St., Ste. 107, San Diego

6 VERBATIM BOOKS
3793 30th St., San Diego

7 WARWICK'S
7812 Girard Ave., La Jolla

GREATER SAN DIEGO

San Diego's the Book Catapult is known for its broad selection of fiction and nonfiction with an emphasis on nature.

The Book Catapult

Once a humble blog, this San Diego mainstay delivers books and community.

I t all started with a blog. Remember those? Seth Marko's love for reading inspired the *Book Catapult*, a blog he founded in 2006 where he reviewed the titles he was reading each week, an online diary of sorts. He gained a large following after San Diego's local radio station KPBS interviewed him about his 117-day reading of a James Patterson novel, an attempt to solve the mystery of why "JPatt" was so popular. Marko concluded that you can "read a chapter in one of [JPatt's] books during a commercial break on American Idol.... [His readers] kind of read by convenience, you know, rather than looking for real literature." After 10 years of blogging about literature, Marko wrote a final post to announce that the *Book Catapult* would become a store. He envisioned it as a place "where you can handle/sniff/flip-through all the books you want...discover books you didn't know you needed to read, maybe have some literature-related conversations."

Today, the Book Catapult is that and more. Located in San Diego's South Park neighborhood, the shop provides a so-called third place—home and work are the first two—vital to nurturing creativity. It is where neighbors meet to converse and to keep informed of local goings-on and where they always feel welcome. It is where local author Susie Ghahremani painted an owl, a squirrel, a sparrow, an opossum, and a raccoon on a colorful mural framing the shelves of the children's section. Longtime regulars, including fans from the days when the Book Catapult was merely a blog, often come by to laugh and gossip alongside newcomers who stop in while visiting the neighborhood's historic Craftsman homes.

THE BOOK CATAPULT
3010B Juniper St., San Diego
thebookcatapult.com

Such activities came to a halt during the pandemic, but both the community and the shop's staff proved their loyalty. Marko and his wife and business partner, Jennifer Powell, say that their business doubled even though the store's front doors were closed to the public. Staff members took online and

SALLOVE

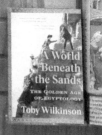

Co-owner Seth Marko's popular book review blog blossomed into this brick-and-mortar store.

phone orders and hand-delivered purchases around the neighborhood more quickly than Amazon.

In the spring of 2022, author events and other in-store gatherings resumed, including the Book Catapult's participation in the popular San Diego Book Crawl, which took place over the last weekend in April and coincided with Indie Bookstore Day. It was an important milestone in the shop's return to normalcy, and Marko and Powell look forward to opening their doors for more celebrations.

Marko likes to say, "If you can find it in an airport bookstore, you probably are not going to find it at the Book Catapult." Instead, you will find such riches as literary fiction, independent-press releases, works in translation, and non-fiction with an emphasis on nature.

In other words, no JPatt. ∎

—AMY E. WALLEN

ARTIFACT BOOKS
603 S. Coast Hwy. 101, Encinitas
artifactrarebooks.com

Artifact Books offers everything from used, beach-read paperbacks to rare collectibles and signed first editions. Antiquarian poetry collections from the 17th century share the shelves with new releases and popular thrillers. The store offers a distinctive book-buying experience that includes special celebrations, themed sales, and author signing events.

LIBÉLULA
950 S. 26th St., San Diego
libelulabooksandco.com

Like the dragonfly the bookshop is named after, Libélula inspires dreams in the artistic neighborhood of Barrio Logan. Customers may be greeted by music being played by anyone who cares to sit at the spinet. And in addition to selling used and new books, staff help customers with job applications (a computer is available for online forms), literary explorations, and homework.

MAXWELL'S HOUSE OF BOOKS
8285 La Mesa Blvd., La Mesa
maxwellshouseofbooks.com

Stepping inside Maxwell's House of Books, it's easy to imagine (or remember) what life was like before the internet. Browsing the aisles of secondhand books yields thrilling discoveries in almost any genre. This vintage outpost even has a resident cat, Rorschach, who relishes a scratch behind the ears.

MYSTERIOUS GALAXY
3555 Rosecrans St., Ste. 107, San Diego
mystgalaxy.com

The genre-specific Mysterious Galaxy carries a diverse selection of science fiction books, and its inventory also gives a platform to authors who previously might not have had as much visibility—think: a cookbook section where the books contain recipes from sci-fi, fantasy, and horror worlds.

VERBATIM BOOKS
3793 30th St., San Diego
verbatimbooks.com

Located in the heart of San Diego's North Park neighborhood, Verbatim Books offers shelf space for more than 200 local authors' new titles, a robust secondhand inventory, and a main room reminiscent of an elaborate, gothic-style bower for its readings and other events. In the market for a cool new zine? You'll find plenty of recommendations and samples.

WARWICK'S
7812 Girard Ave., La Jolla
warwicks.com

Founded in 1896, Warwick's is widely known as the country's oldest continuously family-owned bookstore. The events calendar bursts with readings by acclaimed authors, and every week, staff and publisher reps discuss new releases at the shop's virtual Tea Time Recommendations. But what stands out at Warwick's is a knowledgeable staff eager to provide helpful input on any book you might pick up. ■

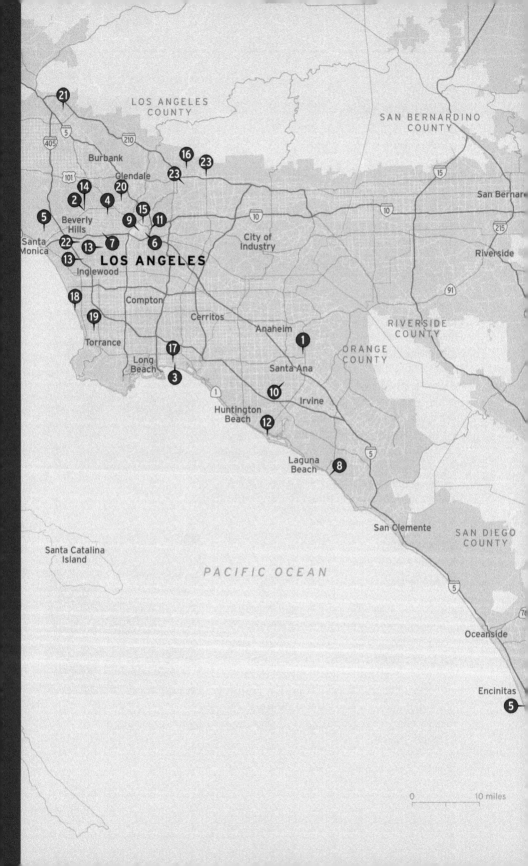

BOOKSTORES | LEGEND

1 **BOOK CARNIVAL**
348 S. Tustin St., Orange

2 **BOOK SOUP**
8818 Sunset Blvd., West Hollywood

3 **CASITA BOOKSTORE**
1440 E. 4th St., Long Beach

4 **CHEVALIER'S BOOKS**
133 N. Larchmont Blvd., Los Angeles

5 **DIESEL, A BOOKSTORE**
225 26th St., Ste. 33, Santa Monica
12843 El Camino Real, Ste. 104, San Diego

6 **HENNESSEY + INGALLS**
300 S. Santa Fe Ave., Ste. M, Los Angeles

7 **LA LIBRERÍA**
4732½ W. Washington Blvd., Los Angeles

8 **LAGUNA BEACH BOOKS**
1200 S. Coast Hwy., Laguna Beach

9 **THE LAST BOOKSTORE**
453 S. Spring St., Fl. G, Los Angeles

10 **LIBROMOBILE**
1150 S. Bristol St., Ste. A3, Santa Ana

11 **LIBROS SCHMIBROS**
103 N. Boyle Ave., Los Angeles

12 **LIDO VILLAGE BOOKS**
3424 Via Lido, Ste. 101, Newport Beach

13 **MALIK BOOKS**
6000 Sepulveda Blvd., Ste. 2470, Culver City
3650 W. Martin Luther King Jr. Blvd.,
Ste. 245, Los Angeles

14 **MYSTERY PIER BOOKS**
8826 Sunset Blvd., West Hollywood

15 **NOW SERVING**
727 N. Broadway, Ste. 133, Los Angeles

16 **OCTAVIA'S BOOKSHELF**
1361 N. Hill Ave., Pasadena

17 **PAGE AGAINST THE MACHINE**
2714 E. 4th St., Long Beach

18 **PAGES**
904 Manhattan Ave., Manhattan Beach

19 **SANDPIPER BOOKS**
4665 Torrance Blvd., Torrance

20 **SKYLIGHT BOOKS**
1818 N. Vermont Ave., Los Angeles

21 **TÍA CHUCHA'S CENTRO CULTURAL & BOOKSTORE**
12677 Glenoaks Blvd., Sylmar

22 **VILLAGE WELL BOOKS & COFFEE**
9900 Culver Blvd., Ste. 1B, Culver City

23 **VROMAN'S BOOKSTORE**
695 E. Colorado Blvd., Pasadena
3729 E. Foothill Blvd., Pasadena

LOS ANGELES AREA

A concrete planter in the middle of Skylight Books provides for additional seating during the shop's popular author events.

Skylight Books

Inspired window displays set the tone for one of Los Angeles's most inclusive literary hot spots.

O n a block of North Vermont Avenue, between the Dresden Room lounge and the Los Feliz Theater, you will find Skylight Books, a shop with some of the country's most intriguing window displays. They aren't especially flashy or artfully composed, but they're reliable evidence of Skylight's wide-ranging, inclusive, curatorial spirit. On a recent visit, among the few dozen showcased books were H. Melt's poetry collection, *There Are Trans People Here*; Akwaeke Emezi's cerebral, surreal novel *Freshwater*; and *Memorias de un Abedul*, the Spanish-language version of *Memories of a Birch Tree*, Daniel Cañas's children's book about persisting in the face of adversity. To encounter the inviting, collective effect and not be beckoned inside is to perhaps lack curiosity about humanity. Mary Williams, Skylight's general manager, says, "We really do try to have the book that you're looking for and also something that you didn't know that you wanted."

SKYLIGHT BOOKS
1818 N. Vermont Ave.,
Los Angeles
skylightbooks.com

Skylight has been a hub for booklovers of all kinds since 1996, when its store-opening celebration included Wanda Coleman, John Rechy, Hubert Selby Jr., and Flea from the Red Hot Chili Peppers. Visiting the shop, and sitting inside on the circular, polished concrete planter at its center, feels like placing yourself at the vanguard of Southern California literary life (an impression that intensifies if one factors in the space's previous decades as Chatterton's Bookshop, an important venue for Los Angeles poetry). The planter contains a ficus tree, its slender, leafy branches stretching across the diamond-patterned rafters and pressing against the store's high, eponymous skylight.

Throughout its existence, Skylight Books has maintained a robust in-store reading schedule that has welcomed, with equal enthusiasm, renowned locals

such as Susan Straight or Janet Fitch, touring luminaries such as Joyce Carol Oates or David Mitchell, countless emerging authors promoting debut books, and MFA writing students giving their first public readings. For many, seeing one's name neatly written in chalk on the sidewalk signboard of upcoming events is a rite of passage, an indication that one has truly made it.

And for audience members, to find a seat in the three rows of folding chairs or a spot against the rolling shelves of self-help and Eastern philosophy stock (pushed to the side to accommodate as many standing-room-only folks as possible) is to partake in one of the city's best, ongoing book parties. Readings occasionally include Franny, the shop's current free-roaming cat, employed since 2009 (rest in peace, Lucy), and are regularly hosted by the inimitable Noel Alumit, novelist and longtime employee. Favorites among the hundreds of events he's hosted? "A posthumous tribute to Toni Morrison," Alumit recalls. "She had just died, and the community needed to mourn her." And a gathering with British novelist Jeanette Winterson. "It was her first literary event in Los Angeles, and I had the opportunity to introduce her!"

When visiting, be sure to also allot some time to stop by the Arts Annex, Skylight's adjacent storefront, formerly Colonial Drug & Surgical Supply. The Arts Annex's stockpiles of comics, graphic novels, and art books, some distributed in the United States exclusively by Skylight, will surely inspire giddy, sugared excitement. ∎

—MICHAEL JAIME-BECERRA

Author and activist Luis J. Rodriguez cofounded Tía Chucha's Centro Cultural & Bookstore to nurture creativity and imagination in his neighborhood.

Tía Chucha's Centro Cultural & Bookstore

This dynamic cultural center constantly evolves for the benefit of its community.

Roughly 23 years ago, poet, critic, and activist Luis J. Rodriguez noticed a particular discrepancy between the northeast San Fernando Valley he calls home and other California regions of similar population size: his corner of the Valley lacked any significant art-and-culture center or community space. Rodriguez, who knew the impact art and writing can have on impoverished neighborhoods—he credits books with helping him out of a life of crime and gang violence—hoped to provide a creative outlet to locals.

The idea for an organization to cultivate an artistic community, provide mentors to younger generations within and outside the arts, and inspire imaginations in San Fernando was quickly born. Rodriguez teamed up with his wife, Trini, and brother-in-law Enrique Sanchez to launch Tía Chucha's, a café and bookstore named after Rodriguez's high-spirited and creative aunt, in 2001.

TÍA CHUCHA'S CENTRO CULTURAL & BOOKSTORE
12677 Glenoaks Blvd., Sylmar
tiachucha.org

"We opened up a space where people could come out of the woodwork," recalls Rodriguez. "The lady who sold tamales was a great singer, and she would come to our open mics. There was a waiter at this restaurant who, it turned out, was a great poet from Mexico."

Throughout the years, Tía Chucha's evolved to better meet the needs of the community, as any good cultural center is prone to do. The café was closed, and the bookstore was expanded and rolled into Tía Chucha's nonprofit arm (established in 2003), which eventually landed in Sylmar.

Tucked into a corner of a bustling shopping center, the new space was designed by Sanchez and others to fulfill various functions on a day-to-day basis. The back half of the main room has been a stage for occasional open mic nights, the setting for author meet and greets, and a background for TikTok videos.

During one finals week, the area was even furnished with desks to give local students a peaceful environment to work in, recounts Sarahi Sepulveda, one of Tía Chucha's bookstore assistants.

The rows of books for sale further reveal the ideals of the establishment. Information about social justice movements, Indigenous art, and Aztec patterns can be found in many of them, alongside work by local authors. Indigenous novels and poetry collections are prominent on the left side of the shop. To the right, a robust shelf bears the label "Luis J. Rodriguez" and features myriad works by the Tía Chucha's cofounder. Another, branded with "Tía Chucha's Press," is laden with books from the center's publishing wing.

For those looking to establish roots, Tía Chucha's has an internship program that offers chosen applicants two paths: one focused on public program-

ming and the other on bookstore operations. Karen M. Ugarte started at Tía Chucha's as an intern; she is now the bookstore manager.

With a large gathering space, charismatic staff members, and a lot of innovative ideas, Tía Chucha's Centro Cultural & Bookstore is the space Rodriguez envisioned decades ago.

"We have a very poor community, and yet the people are rich in their language, in their culture, in their traditions—and I think we really need to build on that richness," says Rodriguez. "It's interesting that in many neighborhoods you can buy any gun, any liquor, any drug you want, but you can't buy a book. You know what I'm saying? Cultural spaces are necessary. We need a Tía Chucha's–like place in every neighborhood." ∎

—Elizabeth Casillas

BOOK CARNIVAL
348 S. Tustin St., Orange
annesbookcarnival.com

Get your murders here, folks! It's not fancy (think '70s-strip-mall aesthetic), but for some 40 years, Book Carnival has been killing it with mystery, suspense, and crime fiction fans in north Orange County. It's the place to catch readings by some of the genres' big dogs, from Michael Connelly to Faye Kellerman, or to join a book club.

BOOK SOUP
8818 Sunset Blvd., West Hollywood
booksoup.com

On the Sunset Strip's western edge, a stone's throw from the Viper Room and the Whisky a Go Go, this shop boasts of being a bookseller to the great and infamous. True to its word, it is probably the only place in the world where you can see Harvey Fierstein and Joan Collins discuss their respective memoirs in the same week.

CASITA BOOKSTORE
1440 E. 4th St., Long Beach
casitabooks.com

Half a block west of Fourth Street's vibrant Retro Row, Casita Bookstore offers a varied selection that reflects Long Beach's diverse communities, from Spanish-language children's books to novels by Black and LGBTQ authors, with a focus on readers 12 and under. Befitting its name, the homey place has the look and feel of a casita, a little house. Regular events include story times and book signings with children's authors.

CHEVALIER'S BOOKS
133 N. Larchmont Blvd., Los Angeles
chevaliersbooks.com

Located in the tony neighborhood of
Larchmont Village, this shop offers an
eclectic selection of contemporary fiction and
nonfiction, along with a modest but inviting
children's section. A long, low shelf spotlights
books intended to catch little eyes, like *The
ABCs of Socialism* and a *Hip Hop Family
Tree*.

DIESEL, A BOOKSTORE
225 26th St., Ste. 33, Santa Monica
12843 El Camino Real, Ste. 104, San Diego
dieselbookstore.com

Tucked within Santa Monica's picturesque
open-air Brentwood Country Mart,
Diesel boasts a multitude of genres within
its compact, cozy space. With detailed
recommendation tabs adorning each section
for quiet browsers and insightful staff
members eager to chat with shoppers who want to talk books, visitors can
rest assured they will be guided comfortably toward their next read.

HENNESSEY + INGALLS
300 S. Santa Fe Ave., Ste. M, Los Angeles
hennesseyingalls.com

From the ground floor of a block-long
apartment complex in Downtown's Arts
District, Hennessey + Ingalls focuses solely on
books about the visual arts. Sections include
Industrial Design, Architecture Theory,
and Photo Technique. The well-stocked
newsstand is one of the last places to find
current copies of *Juxtapoz*.

LA LIBRERÍA
4732½ W. Washington Blvd., Los Angeles
la-libreria.net

This Mid City destination is the only bookstore in the city of Los Angeles that exclusively sells Spanish-language children's books. Many are sourced from independent presses in Latin America and Spain. Need help deciding what to buy? Request a copy of *262 Children's Books to Read in Spanish*, the store's free catalog of recommendations.

LAGUNA BEACH BOOKS
1200 S. Coast Hwy., Laguna Beach
lagunabeachbooks.com

If a major author is touring, chances are their Orange County stop will include, if not be limited to, this neighborhood institution on the Pacific Coast Highway. Laguna Beach Books is a narrow but long store featuring classics, upmarket fiction as well as blockbusters, and more—not to mention a great nod to books on surf and skate culture.

THE LAST BOOKSTORE
453 S. Spring St., Fl. G, Los Angeles
lastbookstorela.com

Housed in the former Crocker Citizens Bank building, this Downtown bookshop has ample new and used stock on the first floor. But don't skip the upstairs: shelves stuffed with sci-fi, the Danger Room of comics, and an actual vault filled with enough true crime and horror to inspire the next *Saw* movie are just a taste of what awaits. (Bonus points if you spot French street artist Invader's piece out front.)

LIBROMOBILE

1150 S. Bristol St., Ste. A3, Santa Ana
libromobile.com

LibroMobile founder Sarah Rafael García wanted a place where BIPOC folks could see their stories on the shelves and their art on the walls. First a books-on-wheels operation, LibroMobile has become far more: a brick-and-mortar store with a section dedicated to local authors and another for BIPOC art, making it clear that this is a place for the community made possible by the community.

LIBROS SCHMIBROS

103 N. Boyle Ave., Los Angeles
librosschmibros.org

Across the street from Mariachi Plaza stands Libros Schmibros, a bilingual lending library in the historic Chicano neighborhood of Boyle Heights. Since its opening in 2010, this local institution has focused on providing books to the surrounding community, regardless of readers' means. Libros Schmibros also hosts podcasts and community events and runs a fellowship program for high school students.

LIDO VILLAGE BOOKS

3424 Via Lido, Ste. 101, Newport Beach
lidovillagebooks.com

Tiny but mighty is this elegant indie, tucked into the sleek waterside development of Lido Marina Village. When the longtime owners of Lido Village Books decided to retire, Michelle Pierce saved the day by buying the shop, maintaining its reputation for an exquisitely curated selection for the well-read (or those who want to be), and promoting open readings for local writers.

MALIK BOOKS

6000 Sepulveda Blvd., Ste. 2470, Culver City
3650 W. Martin Luther King Jr. Blvd., Ste. 245,
Los Angeles
malikbooks.com

One might not expect to find a repository
for Black literary achievement and joy at the
Westfield Culver City mall, but nevertheless,
Malik Books proudly endures just steps away
from the food court. The poster-size placards
touting milestones in Black history aren't for sale, but the vibrant cross
section of books, by iconic and lesser-known Black authors, definitely is.

MYSTERY PIER BOOKS

8826 Sunset Blvd., West Hollywood
mysterypierbooks.com

Mystery Pier is one of the state's best places to
secure rare first editions of classics by writers
like Hemingway, Nabokov, and Austen (fair
warning: that original printing of *Emma* will
set you back $40,000). Hollywood legends
have long been drawn by the shop's collection,
including its wide selection of original movie
scripts, many signed by the casts.

NOW SERVING

727 N. Broadway, Ste. 133, Los Angeles
nowservingla.com

Concentrating on culinary arts, this
Chinatown bookseller invites a wanderlust
for global cuisines. Consider the additional
selection of chef Joyce Chen's scissors and
appreciate the framed poster of the late food
critic Jonathan Gold's dining rules. The wall
of food periodicals may immediately activate
subscription impulses. It seems impossible to leave Now Serving without
wanting to eat—and you may even be inspired to cook.

OCTAVIA'S BOOKSHELF
1361 N. Hill Ave., Pasadena
octaviasbookshelf.com

Pasadena's first independent bookstore owned by a Black woman opened its doors in February 2023. Octavia's Bookshelf founder Nikki High hadn't encountered science fiction featuring Black stories until she read the work of Pasadena native Octavia E. Butler as a teenager. She created this cozy eponymous bookstore to feature the work of BIPOC authors and give younger generations the opportunity to see themselves reflected in literature.

PAGE AGAINST THE MACHINE
2714 E. 4th St., Long Beach
patmbooks.com

Named in honor of Los Angeles–based rock band Rage Against the Machine, Page Against the Machine opened in 2019 and thrives as a home to books on subjects such as activism and political movements, socially conscious theory, and sustainability. This one-room shop, just four minutes from Long Beach City Beach, is where revolutions begin.

PAGES
904 Manhattan Ave., Manhattan Beach
pagesabookstore.com

Located just a couple of blocks from the water, this woman-owned bookstore hosts author events, weekly story times, and book clubs for all ages. With its signature blue walls and the sea breeze drifting through the shop, Pages is a great place to find your next beach read.

SANDPIPER BOOKS
4665 Torrance Blvd., Torrance
facebook.com/people
/sandpiperbooks/100064693238501

This unassuming bookstore has something
for everyone. From the dollar and two-dollar
finds competing for space in the roller cart
outside the shop to the wall of out-of-print
and collector's titles, Sandpiper Books is
an old-school gem, with plenty of writerly
trinkets to boot.

VILLAGE WELL BOOKS & COFFEE
9900 Culver Blvd., Ste. 1B, Culver City
villagewell.com

It's been open only since 2021, but Village
Well is already a major community gathering
spot, with its airy and expansive café and
diverse slate of poetry readings and author
appearances. Owner Jennifer Caspar puts
an emphasis on social justice issues through
educational programs and on-site events.

VROMAN'S BOOKSTORE
695 E. Colorado Blvd., Pasadena
3729 E. Foothill Blvd., Pasadena
vromansbookstore.com

Founded in 1894 by Adam Clark Vroman, a
relocated midwesterner, this well-appointed
shop is Southern California's oldest
bookseller. Vroman's is beloved throughout
the San Gabriel Valley for its robust English-
language children's section, an abundance
of discounted jewels in its clearance section, and plenty of free parking out
back at its Colorado Boulevard location. (Tip for writers: Vroman's offers a
discount to authors needing copies of their own book.) ∎

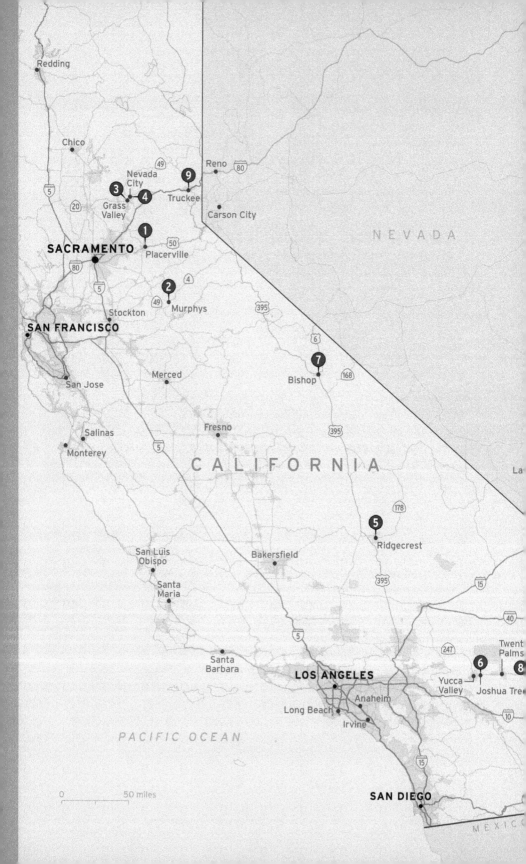

BOOKSTORES | LEGEND

1 **THE BOOKERY**
326 Main St., Placerville

2 **BOOKS ON MAIN**
416 Main St., Murphys

3 **BOOKTOWN BOOKS**
107 Bank St., Grass Valley

4 **HARMONY BOOKS**
130 Main St., Nevada City

5 **RED ROCK BOOKS**
206 W. Ridgecrest Blvd., Ridgecrest

6 **SPACE COWBOY BOOKS**
61871 Twentynine Palms Hwy., Joshua Tree

7 **SPELLBINDER BOOKS**
124 S. Main St., Bishop

8 **WONDERLAND BOOKS**
83100 Amboy Rd., Twentynine Palms

9 **WORD AFTER WORD**
10052 Donner Pass Rd., Truckee

DESERT/SIERRA

Jean-Paul L. Garnier opened Space Cowboy Books in the town of Joshua Tree in 2016. It's the only dedicated bookstore in the surrounding 37 square miles of desert.

Space Cowboy Books

Joshua Tree's only bookstore is from a galaxy far, far away.

hat makes the deserts and mountains of eastern California so wonderfully different from the coast and valleys is the lack of people and abundance of public land, best represented by a wild paradise of national parks and monuments and forests from the High Sierra to Death Valley to Joshua Tree.

Since the days of Mary Hunter Austin and John Muir, this immense solitude of mountains and deserts has been especially appreciated by readers, writers, and other accidental philosophers. The small-town backcountry bookstores are cherished in these parts.

Jean-Paul L. Garnier opened Space Cowboy Books in the town of Joshua Tree in 2016, within a funky little homegrown mall called Sun Alley Shops—a convenient two-minute walk from the Joshua Tree Saloon, itself on the winding two-lane road that leads into Joshua Tree National Park. Local gift shops usually have a collection of tourist guides, but Space Cowboy remains the only dedicated bookstore in this sprawling Mojave Desert community of 6,500 people spread over 37 square miles of creosote and sand.

SPACE COWBOY BOOKS
61871 Twentynine Palms Hwy.,
Joshua Tree
spacecowboybooks.com

Space Cowboy is only a few steps away from the tourist-season crowds on Twentynine Palms Highway, but like all the best booksellers, it is a refuge—a whimsical refuge, in this case, with a plywood space alien pointing the way inside and a satisfying selection of new, used, and locally authored books filling the compact space. Garnier's collection of Star Wars figurines and other such sci-fi trinkets watch over the shelves, while Garnier can usually be found behind the tiny counter in back—where, in keeping with his shop's name, he wears his western hat indoors.

Space Cowboy is deeply involved in its community, as a good local bookshop should be. Garnier works with local schools and Copper Mountain College on projects such as literary readings and library donations, and the back patio of Sun Alley Shops has a stage and seating for the store's author events and

science fiction screenings, including silent classics scored with live music. The most labor-intensive work is the media Space Cowboy itself produces, in the form of the sci-fi podcast *Simultaneous Times* and a growing collection of paperbacks and chapbooks published by Garnier.

Since 2018, *Simultaneous Times* has featured local, regional, and international science fiction authors, playwrights, and poets. The short plays are produced in classic radio-drama style, with original soundtracks, making the podcast unique in a crowded field.

Garnier is an author and poet himself, with several collections to his name, including 2019's Elgin Award–nominated *Future Anthropology*. Like many sci-fi visionaries, he is fascinated by time travel in all its literary and real-life possibilities.

"Books are time machines," Garnier says. "One of the things I love about science fiction is that it's inherently hopeful. By writing about the future, it must be presupposed that there *is* a future. And if there's a future, then there is hope." ∎

—KEN LAYNE

Booktown Books

Lose yourself in this labyrinth of reading pleasures.

By all rights, Booktown Books, the eccentric bookstore and more, should not even exist, much less be thriving. Located in the gold country town of Grass Valley—the middle of nowhere to the uninitiated—the 25-year-old cooperative brings together nine owner-sellers, each offering distinctive merchandise. The much-revered business is more than just a retail-success oddity. When COVID-19 hit, Booktown became a place where people could just go and be—it never closed. "That first month, we had regular customers that called us up and said they had cabin fever: 'Can I come see you in your store?'" Marilyn Tubbs, one of the longest-tenured members, says.

Tubbs and her husband, Tom, obliged, letting visitors browse the well-tended maze of aisles and shelves by appointment while the couple sat outside. Their booths' specialties are regional history and local gardening, but vintage children's and art books can be found as well. "There's so much to view within Booktown Books—try to have a bit of time to view it all," Tubbs advises.

When word spread that Booktown's doors remained open while other businesses were shuttering because of the pandemic, even more folks stopped in, especially those fleeing the Bay Area. "It's been a very hectic last two years," Tubbs says. "It was no longer just the local crowd coming."

BOOKTOWN BOOKS
107 Bank St., Grass Valley
facebook.com/booktownbooks

Housed in a two-story, 4,000-square-foot building that the co-op leased in 2000, Booktown reflects the region's literary affinity and alternative sensibility. One of the West's most productive gold mines was nearby, and the area maintains an Old West ethos tempered by a counterculture vibe and an unusual density of bookstores. (Grass Valley is an internationally designated Book Town, as is nearby Nevada City, also in gold country.)

Other booths at Booktown include An Inner Sanctum, run by another original co-op member, Nicole Dillard, who sells art, music, and cooking titles, and G.F. Wilkinson Books, which focuses on metaphysics and spirituality and carries vintage board games. From his stall, longtimer Tom Cadman sells books about World War II, of which he has one of the largest collections in the region. Anthony and Carly Leano operate From the Land Beyond, peddling graphic novels, comic books, erotica, posters, and rare horror and fantasy DVDs from a large

Located in the gold country town of Grass Valley, Booktown Books is a cooperative that houses nine stalls, each with its own specialty.

room that was once the space of legendary comic book publisher Bud Plant.

There have been as many as 14 owners operating at Booktown at one time. "That was too crowded," Ron "the record guy" Quintana tells me. Quintana's little room just off the entrance feels like a 1990s garage sale stuffed into a shed. The 10-by-15-foot space overflows with yellowing paperbacks, obscure posters, record crates, and placards announcing a "huge $2 CD sale."

Mike Witter, who once owned a bookstore in San Francisco and now has two adjoining rooms in the rear—the most square footage of any member—explains the staffing schedule: "We work in direct proportion to how much space we each have. Some dealers have a lot of books and work three or four days a week, and others have small spaces and work three or four days a month."

Witter specializes in academic texts, and his sections include Hunting & Shooting, Drama, and Nautical. "How many dealers have this much on insects?" he asks, showing off the dedicated shelves. Around the perimeter of the room are framed displays of arrowheads and sharks' teeth. Spine up in rows on a counter are Witter's latest acquisitions, a hardbound collection of the rare bilingual (Latin or Greek plus English) Loeb Classical Library series. "I haven't even priced them yet, but I've already sold about 50, which speaks well of the community here, I think." ∎

—MARCUS CROWDER

  PHOTO BY DAVID CALVERT

THE BOOKERY
326 Main St., Placerville
thebookeryplacerville.com

A locally owned literary institution on U.S. 50 since 1983, Placerville's the Bookery is full of treasures: gold rush and western U.S. history is a specialty. The shop is prized for its customer service and growing selection of occult titles and "weird fiction."

BOOKS ON MAIN
416 Main St., Murphys
booksonmain.net

Along the Highway 4 corridor in Northern California, you'll find the unincorporated town of Murphys, and along its Main Street sits (the aptly named) Books on Main. Even though it's the only dedicated bookstore in Calaveras County, owner Kirsten Gomez manages to stock the hottest fiction on the market. Known for Gomez's personal touch, the shop is also celebrated for its magnificent children's section.

HARMONY BOOKS
130 Main St., Nevada City
loc8nearme.com/california/nevada-city/harmony-books/3172525

Situated off the main street in this old mining town, Harmony Books has brought a new kind of gold to Nevada City's historic assay office. The brick facade, with its hand-painted sign, now welcomes visitors to the only local store that carries new books. Behind a front table dedicated to the latest releases, the shop's shelves are stocked with titles that keep its community in mind.

RED ROCK BOOKS

206 W. Ridgecrest Blvd., Ridgecrest
redrockbooks.net

The only bookshop in Ridgecrest is an expansive 7,000 square feet of new, used, and specialty books (and other gifts) in a welcoming environment—Oliver the cat may greet you—that makes a fine midday stop for eastern California travelers. The local/regional section alone is worth the visit.

SPELLBINDER BOOKS

124 S. Main St., Bishop
instagram.com/spellbinderbooks

Spellbinder has been *the* place for booklovers in the Owens Valley since 1970. Independently owned and stocked with a wide range of fiction, kids' books, nonfiction, and regional titles, this classic stop on the 395 in downtown Bishop also has the Pupfish Cafe, serving coffee and snacks in back.

WONDERLAND BOOKS

83100 Amboy Rd., Twentynine Palms
instagram.com/wonderland.bookshop

A real High Desert experience awaits the book browser at Laura Sibley Bone's Wonderland Books. Open on Sundays and when the flag's up outside, Wonderland is located in a classic homestead cabin across the road from the Palms, a restaurant also owned by the Sibley family. The bar, on quiet afternoons, is a fine place to read whatever you may have picked up at Wonderland.

WORD AFTER WORD
10052 Donner Pass Rd., Truckee
wordafterwordbooks.com

At its downtown location on Donner Pass
Road, where it moved in 2020, Word After
Word offers a wonderfully selected inventory
of new books, including local and regional
titles as well as bestsellers, and a welcoming
kids' room so adults can browse in peace. The
store also operates Rock Cellar Records in the
basement, where it sells vinyl and bargain-priced books. ■

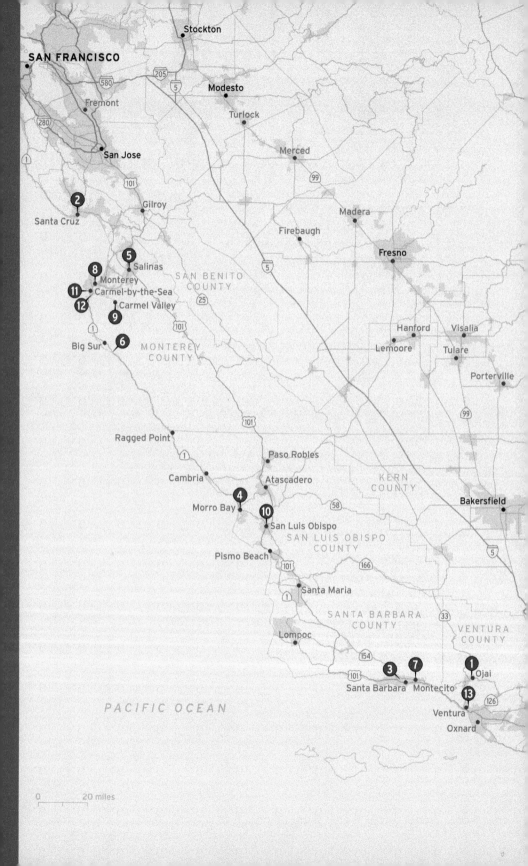

BOOKSTORES | LEGEND

1 BART'S BOOKS
302 W. Matilija St., Ojai

2 BOOKSHOP SANTA CRUZ
1520 Pacific Ave., Santa Cruz

3 CHAUCER'S BOOKS
3321 State St., Santa Barbara

4 COALESCE BOOKSTORE
845 Main St., Morro Bay

5 DOWNTOWN BOOK & SOUND
213 Main St., Salinas

**6 HENRY MILLER
MEMORIAL LIBRARY**
48603 Hwy. 1, Big Sur

7 LOST HORIZON BOOKSTORE
539 San Ysidro Rd., Santa Barbara

8 OLD CAPITOL BOOKS
482 Alvarado St., Monterey

9 OLIVIA & DAISY
13766 Center St., Carmel Valley

10 PHOENIX BOOKS
986 Monterey St., San Luis Obispo

**11 PILGRIM'S WAY BOOKS AND
THE SECRET GARDEN**
Dolores St. between 5th and 6th Aves.,
Carmel-by-the-Sea

12 RIVER HOUSE BOOKS
208 Crossroads Blvd., Carmel

13 TIMBRE BOOKS
1924 E. Main St., Ventura

CENTRAL COAST

Jake Padorr is one of three staff members at the Henry Miller Memorial Library in Big Sur. The bookstore and performance space is situated among the towering redwoods of California's Central Coast.

Henry Miller Memorial Library

At this one-room cultural center, stories come from the trees.

The stretch of California coast known as Big Sur often seems like a place lifted out of a dream. Steep hillsides fall dramatically into a churning sea, and when the fog lies thick between the redwoods, which is often, it can feel like the road has not yet decided where it wants to take you but is making up its mind as you drive.

If you're lucky, the road will take you to the dream-within-a-dream that is the Henry Miller Memorial Library, a bookstore and performance venue established here in 1981 by the writer's friend Emil White just after Miller's death. Step through the tall wooden gate and books are the first things that greet you—rather than sitting quietly on shelves, these books are wrapped in plastic and scattered along the walk that leads to the bookstore. They're set at the bases of redwood trees or propped against the dozen or so art pieces that decorate the grounds. They line the outer walls of the small wooden building and hang from the eaves. Although this unique placement

HENRY MILLER MEMORIAL LIBRARY
48603 Hwy. 1, Big Sur
henrymiller.org

was the library's reaction to COVID (rather than shut down, the shop simply moved the stock outside), there's a certain brazen attitude about the books that seems appropriate, as if they embody the spirit of one of the most audacious writers of the 20th century.

Miller came to Big Sur in 1944 and for almost 20 years lived a few miles down the coast from where the bookstore now resides. With its idyllic surroundings, its exuberant decor, and a culture that encourages visitors to pick up the house guitar or sit down at the piano, the store imparts a sense of grounded excitement. Inside, more books hang from the ceiling, and the place is covered in Miller memorabilia, including movie posters and prints of his paintings; there are also odds and ends like a letter complaining about a photo of the nude backside of White's girlfriend—which is posted beside the offending derrière.

The bottom has good company: Miller is best known for a series of candidly sexual autobiographical novels (including *Tropic of Cancer* and *Tropic of*

Capricorn) written in the 1930s but banned in the United States until 1961. His papers are housed at UCLA and at Yale University, but a back room of the bookstore holds some rare first editions and a small collection of original letters, manuscripts, and paintings that fans have contributed over the years. The small, focused selection of books for sale is curated by Magnus Torén, a former yacht skipper who since 1993 has been the executive director of the nonprofit that runs the library, a de facto cultural center for Big Sur.

Jake Padorr, one of three employees, hosts an open mic night for local talent on the library's outdoor stage, usually on the first Thursday of the month. And bigger acts—such as Patti Smith and Arcade Fire—play small (but pricey) shows there throughout the year.

If the Miller-esque appetite for art and for life is still rare, the bookstore does seem to attract a particular kind of visitor. "People have to go through a couple of filters to get here," Padorr says. "They have to want to get away from phones and technology. Then they have to venture out into this beautiful preserve of nature. Finally, they have to take a leap of faith to walk through this tall fence."

When they do, the spirit of Henry Miller is here to catch them with open arms. ∎

—MARK WALLACE

BART'S BOOKS
302 W. Matilija St., Ojai
bartsbooksojai.com

The open-air shelves of Bart's Books carry an impressive selection, rain or shine, and put one in mind of Paris booksellers' stalls that line the Seine. Books along the street still sell on the honor system, just as they did when Richard "Bart" Bartinsdale first set a few shelves outside his house—still the core of the operation—in 1964.

BOOKSHOP SANTA CRUZ
1520 Pacific Ave., Santa Cruz
bookshopsantacruz.com

This downtown Santa Cruz family-owned establishment packs its high-ceilinged store with a huge collection of titles, culminating in 20,000 square feet of books. And Bookshop Santa Cruz is particularly proud of its local ties cultivated by serving longtime customers and UC Santa Cruz students, as well as a healthy flow of seaside tourists.

CHAUCER'S BOOKS
3321 State St., Santa Barbara
chaucersbooks.com

Spend too much time in Chaucer's and you're liable to walk out with a towering stack of books. Treasures lie around every endcap and line the floors at the foot of the shelves. Every section seems to run deep—even the kids' room. Check the online calendar for a rewarding schedule of virtual and in-person author events.

COALESCE BOOKSTORE
845 Main St., Morro Bay
coalescebookstore.com

This small, inviting shop retains the
supportive, activist vibe in which it was
founded, in 1973, by a recent college grad and
a former Benedictine nun. It has doubled
as a performance space, a publisher, and a
meeting place for women's groups and now
hosts small events in its beautiful chapel
garden.

DOWNTOWN BOOK & SOUND
213 Main St., Salinas
downtownbookandsound.com

Downtown Book & Sound has the
distinction of being the only bookstore
in John Steinbeck's hometown. Owner
Trish Triumpho Sullivan presides over the
establishment's 60,000-plus used and new
books. In addition to Steinbeck's oeuvre,
Downtown sells the author's favorite pencils,
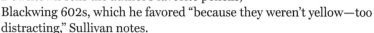
Blackwing 602s, which he favored "because they weren't yellow—too
distracting," Sullivan notes.

LOST HORIZON BOOKSTORE
539 San Ysidro Rd., Santa Barbara
losthorizonbooks.com

Serendipity is the word at this store for
book collectors of all stripes. From pricey
antiquarian volumes to Californiana, rare
sci-fi first editions, and interesting, reasonably
priced books you'll find nowhere else, Lost
Horizon offers a distinctive selection that also
includes prints and original comic book art.

OLD CAPITOL BOOKS
482 Alvarado St., Monterey
oldcapitolbooks.com

Located on historic Alvarado Street in
Monterey, Old Capitol Books hosts open mic
readings and has a decidedly political tilt,
sponsoring an Anarchist Reading Group.
Owner Ali Elfaki and bookseller Stephanie
Spoto offer everything from titles on social
theory to erotica.

OLIVIA & DAISY
13766 Center St., Carmel Valley
oliviaanddaisy.com

This charming Carmel Valley establishment
is a magnet for local literati and wine country
visitors alike. Founded in 2021 by former
Orinda Books owner Maria Roden and
designer Jane Pakis, it has Europa and New
York Review editions, coffee-table books,
and much more and hosts readings with
neighbors like Pulitzer Prize winner Jane Smiley.

PHOENIX BOOKS
986 Monterey St., San Luis Obispo
instagram.com/phoenixbooksslo

The best used bookstores do their jobs
quietly, putting just the right title in your
hands seemingly by magic. Phoenix is a great
example—packed with unexpected finds, it
serves as a portal to many cultures, moods,
and modes of thought, its shelves always
ready with that perfect book you didn't know
you needed.

PILGRIM'S WAY BOOKS AND THE SECRET GARDEN
Dolores St. between 5th and 6th Aves.,
Carmel-by-the-Sea
pilgrimsway.com

Browse candles and incense beneath a geodesic dome surrounded by Buddhas and fountains in this little shop's Zen garden. Inside, inspirational literature and contemporary and regional titles join crystals, tarot decks, and polished stones. Owners Paul Fridlund and Cynthia Fernandes met and married here over 20 years ago and still maintain the spiritual oasis with care.

RIVER HOUSE BOOKS
208 Crossroads Blvd., Carmel
riverhousebookscarmel.com

Carmel residents drew a sigh of relief when Scott and Jennifer Lund, who also own Lula's Chocolates across the street, stepped in to save River House Books in 2018 after the then-owners announced their retirement. The well-appointed store features fiction, travel titles, California histories, magazines—and a killer mystery section. It also sells Peepers reading glasses!

TIMBRE BOOKS
1924 E. Main St., Ventura
timbrebooks.com

This indie neighborhood bookstore has a Murakami vibe, from the vintage typewriter at the front ("Type us a note!") to the cool jazz spinning on the turntable. Locals come in from Singing Sun coffee shop next door to hang out and browse the store's imaginatively curated selection, which includes memoirs, graphic novels, and a section devoted to "antiracism & history." ∎

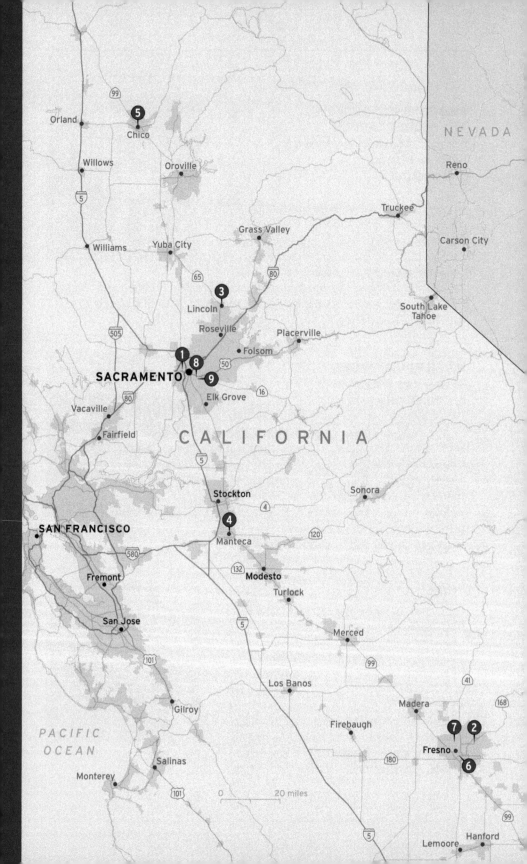

BOOKSTORES | LEGEND

1 BEERS BOOKS
915 S St., Sacramento

2 A BOOK BARN
640 Clovis Ave., Clovis

3 THE BOOK CELLAR
96 Lincoln Blvd., Lincoln

4 THE BOOK EXCHANGE
332 N. Main St., Manteca

5 THE BOOKSTORE
118 Main St., Chico

6 HART'S HAVEN
950 N. Van Ness Ave., Fresno

7 PETUNIA'S PLACE
6027 N. Palm Ave., Fresno

8 UNDERGROUND BOOKS
2814 35th St., Sacramento

9 WILD SISTERS BOOK CO.
3960 60th St., Sacramento

CENTRAL VALLEY

Underground Books is
located in Sacramento's
Oak Park neighborhood.
Specialties include books by
Black authors and titles on
Black culture and history.

Underground Books

This anchor of a Sacramento neighborhood filled the void left by the local library's closure.

A single book can bloom a community, and a thoughtful bookstore can sustain its growth. Underground Books—rooted in the historically Black neighborhood of Oak Park in Sacramento—is a nonprofit bookstore whose curatorial brilliance partners beauty with meaning, soul with optimism.

Founded in 2003, Underground is managed by Georgia "Mother Rose" West, under whose leadership it functions as a community hub. "We are connected," she says. "We try to do anything and everything." The store hosts free events like readings, author signings, and community discussions, and on its stunning Instagram page, Mother Rose highlights a Book of the Week. Both in-store and online, you'll find books like *My Grandmother's Hands*, by Resmaa Menakem, and *The Other Black Girl*, by Zakiya Dalila Harris, as well as handmade cards and T-shirts with "Young, Gifted & Black" printed brightly on them.

UNDERGROUND BOOKS
2814 35th St., Sacramento
underground-books.indiecommerce.com

In the predominantly conservative Central Valley, Underground Books stands out because its programming and inventory uplift stories of people and communities that have historically been marginalized and invisibilized in places like Sacramento, Merced, Gustine, Dos Palos, and Parlier—just a few of the towns that make up California's fruit basket. It's not only a place to buy books—it's a transformative space and project rooted in the restoration of community and the preservation of the area residents' dignity. In the 1970s, the only library in Oak Park closed, limiting people's access to books. In 2003, Underground Books was born through the efforts of St. Hope, a network of local nonprofits. Cassandra Jennings, the president and CEO of St. Hope, has

Founded in 2003, Underground Books is managed by Georgia "Mother Rose" West.

said, "If the community doesn't benefit, then we are doing something wrong."

In many ways, Underground's sheer presence is power. It's a place for Black people to gather and to learn and to be proud, and a place for non-Black people to gather and learn and grow. After the murders of George Floyd, Ahmaud Arbery, and countless others, and the particularly clear confrontations with anti-Blackness in the United States that followed, books have proved to be doors to our innermost houses. Mother Rose calls her own education in Black history an awakening and sees her 26 years as a registered nurse as her own unique path to wanting to reach people through Underground Books. "There is so much rich history to help you broaden your education if you knew about some of these people and these things that have happened, because you are not learning the whole history of the United States in your classes," she says. "So if you really want to learn and have a heart for learning, there is something in this bookstore for you."

Underground provides internships and employment to high school students, organizes an annual Juneteenth Block Party, and hosts Let's Read Oak Park—an interactive book reading for elementary school children with an emphasis on cultural themes. Kids who attend this free monthly event receive a book of their choice on the house. Families gather at the bookstore for activities like Christmas in Oak Park, where in 2021 a Black Santa rolled up on a motorcycle. "The kids were all jumping up and down and were lined up around the block," Mother Rose recalls, adding, "We are about community. It is just amazing. We love it." ∎

—SARA BORJAS

BEERS BOOKS
915 S St., Sacramento
beersbooks.com

Founded in 1936, Beers Books has passed
through four generations of ownership and
continues to flourish in the digital age. The
store is open daily for folks who want an
in-person experience and love used books;
it partners with Bookshop.org to bring
new books and special orders to its online
shoppers.

A BOOK BARN
640 Clovis Ave., Clovis
clovisbookbarn.com

Located in the center of Old Town Clovis,
one of the San Joaquin Valley's largest used
booksellers looks like a cross between a Wild
West emporium and saloon. A Book Barn
houses around 100,000 to 125,000 books in-
store and between 1 million and 1.5 million
in a warehouse for online sales.

THE BOOK CELLAR
96 Lincoln Blvd., Lincoln
facebook.com/mybookcellar

Books are a "magical escape," says Debbie
Swindler, who founded this tiny shop. The
entrance is adorned with opening lines from
the Harry Potter series—next to a wooden
portal into the children's section. For adults:
fiction meticulously arranged by genre.

THE BOOK EXCHANGE
332 N. Main St., Manteca
facebook.com/bookexchangemantecaca

Swap old loves for new ones at the Book
Exchange. The shop offers generous store
credit for used books and has amassed a
trove of general-interest titles as well as
romance novels, children's books, and esoteric
collections like Stargate and Ellora's Cave
erotica.

THE BOOKSTORE
118 Main St., Chico
chicobooks.com

The Instagram post captioned "Another
stunning find! A signed *Dune*? Whaaat!!?"
captures the vibe of this college-town oasis.
Events like Valentine's Day poetry-on-demand
reflect the perspective of co-owners Muir
Hughes and husband Josh Mills: bookstores
are essential to a strong community.

HART'S HAVEN
950 N. Van Ness Ave., Fresno
facebook.com/hartshavenbooks

Hart's Haven, based in the soul of Fresno—
the Tower District—is a longtime supporter
of and host to Fresno's LitHop and Rogue
festivals. The store includes a stage where
poetry heavy hitters like Juan Felipe Herrera
and Joseph Rios have performed their work.

PETUNIA'S PLACE
6027 N. Palm Ave., Fresno
petuniasbooks.com

The most thoughtful books and gifts for kids from all backgrounds can be bought at Petunia's Place, a delicately curated children's and YA retailer. Owner Jean Fennacy, an educator, is a lifelong advocate for children's literacy.

WILD SISTERS BOOK CO.
3960 60th St., Sacramento
wildsistersbookco.com

Drop by this lovely South Sac shop with your little ones, who are encouraged to write a letter to the bookstore fairy, or leave them at home and indulge your own literary needs at one of Wild Sisters' recurring Boozy Book Fairs, hosted at local taprooms. Sisters Claire Bone and Noelle Baganz's bookstore also offers story time, book clubs, and store credit for secondhand titles. ∎

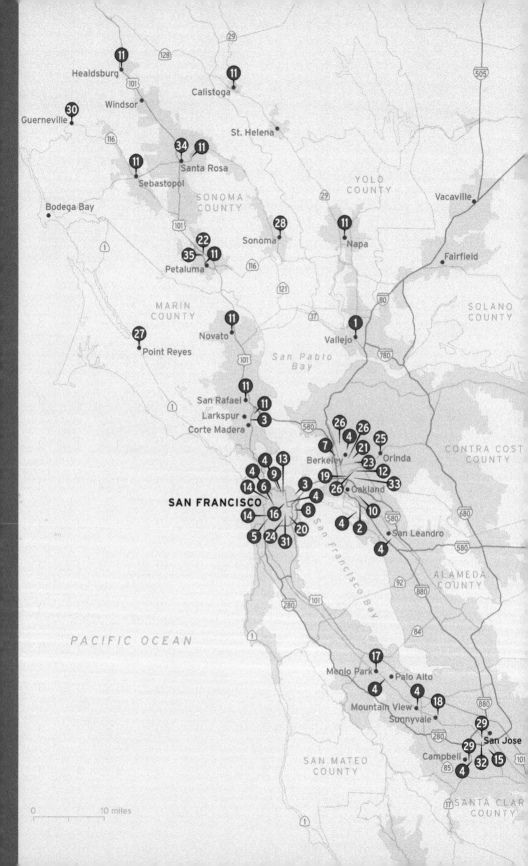

BOOKSTORES | LEGEND

1 **ALIBI BOOKSHOP**
624 Marin St., Vallejo

2 **BANDUNG BOOKS**
2289 International Blvd., Oakland

3 **BOOK PASSAGE**
51 Tamal Vista Blvd., Corte Madera
1 Ferry Building, San Francisco

4 **BOOKS INC.**
601 Van Ness Ave., San Francisco
3515 California St., San Francisco
2251 Chestnut St., San Francisco
1491 Shattuck Ave., Berkeley
1344 Park St., Alameda
2483 Washington Ave., San Leandro
74 Town & Country Village, Palo Alto
317 Castro St., Mountain View
1875 S. Bascom Ave., Ste. 600, Campbell

5 **BOOKSHOP WEST PORTAL**
80 West Portal Ave., San Francisco

6 **THE BOOKSMITH**
1727 Haight St., San Francisco

7 **BUILDERS BOOKSOURCE**
1817 4th St., Berkeley

8 **CHRISTOPHER'S BOOKS**
1400 18th St., San Francisco

9 **CITY LIGHTS BOOKSELLERS & PUBLISHERS**
261 Columbus Ave., San Francisco

10 **THE COLLECTIVE OAKLAND**
811 Broadway, Oakland

11 **COPPERFIELD'S BOOKS**
138 N. Main St., Sebastopol
104 Matheson St., Healdsburg
1330 Lincoln Ave., Calistoga
775 Village Ct., Santa Rosa
140 Kentucky St., Petaluma
1300 1st St., Ste. 398, Napa
999 Grant Ave., Ste. 105, Novato
1200 4th St., San Rafael
2419 Larkspur Landing Circle, Larkspur

12 **EAST BAY BOOKSELLERS**
5433 College Ave., Oakland

13 **FOREST BOOKS**
1748 Buchanan St., San Francisco

14 **GREEN APPLE BOOKS**
506 Clement St., San Francisco
1231 9th Ave., San Francisco

15 **HICKLEBEE'S**
1378 Lincoln Ave., San Jose

16 **ISOTOPE: THE COMIC BOOK LOUNGE**
326 Fell St., San Francisco

17 **KEPLER'S BOOKS & MAGAZINES**
1010 El Camino Real, Ste. 100, Menlo Park

18 **LEIGH'S FAVORITE BOOKS**
121 S. Murphy Ave., Sunnyvale

19 **MARCUS BOOKS**
3900 Martin Luther King Jr. Way, Oakland

20 **MEDICINE FOR NIGHTMARES BOOKSTORE & GALLERY**
3036 24th St., San Francisco

21 **MOE'S BOOKS**
2476 Telegraph Ave., Berkeley

22 **MORTI'S USED BOOK NOOK AND CAT ADOPTION LOUNGE**
2200 Petaluma Blvd. N., Ste. 500, Petaluma

23 **MRS. DALLOWAY'S LITERARY AND GARDEN ARTS**
2904 College Ave., Berkeley

24 **OMNIVORE BOOKS ON FOOD**
3885A Cesar Chavez St., San Francisco

25 **ORINDA BOOKS**
276 Village Square, Orinda

26 **PEGASUS BOOKS**
2349 Shattuck Ave., Berkeley
1855 Solano Ave., Berkeley
5560 College Ave., Oakland

27 **POINT REYES BOOKS**
11315 Hwy. 1, Point Reyes Station

28 **READERS' BOOKS**
130 E. Napa St., Sonoma

29 **RECYCLE BOOKSTORE**
275 E. Campbell Ave., Campbell
1066 the Alameda, San Jose

30 **RUSSIAN RIVER BOOKS & LETTERS**
14045 Armstrong Woods Rd., Guerneville

31 **SILVER SPROCKET**
1018 Valencia St., San Francisco

32 **SPACECAT**
1415 W. San Carlos St., San Jose

33 **SPECTATOR BOOKS**
4163 Piedmont Ave., Oakland

34 **TREEHORN BOOKS**
625 4th St., Santa Rosa

35 **WORD HORDE EMPORIUM OF THE WEIRD & FANTASTIC**
2200 Petaluma Blvd. N., Ste. 805, Petaluma

BAY AREA

Founded in 1960, Marcus Books is the longest continuously operating Black-owned bookstore in the United States. Its founders viewed books and the struggle for Black self-determination as deeply connected.

Marcus Books

The nation's oldest Black-owned bookseller is still here—and thriving.

E ntering Marcus Books, the nation's longest continuously operating independent Black bookstore, is like stepping into living U.S. history. The shop occupies a corner on Martin Luther King Jr. Way in West Oakland. Outside, a faded mural on the garage next to the brick storefront depicts the Bay Bridge, a map of Africa in the colors of the Black Liberation flag, and the aphorism "The answer is N us. The world changes when we do." Rising from the sidewalk, a series of more-vibrant murals span the right side of the building, featuring Marcus Garvey, the Black Nationalist and Pan-Africanist leader for whom the store is named; Malcolm X; Marcus Books founders Drs. Julian and Raye Richardson; and an African drummer. Beside these figures are painted the spines of books by such luminaries as Toni Morrison, James Baldwin, and Maya Angelou (all of whom visited the shop) and several children, relaxing and reading. The interior is equally inspiring. African art and posters of political and cultural figures like Dr. King, Sojourner Truth, Paul Robeson, and B.B. King cover the walls, while bookcases and tables stacked with books are scattered throughout the room. One section is

MARCUS BOOKS
3900 Martin Luther King Jr. Way,
Oakland
marcusbooks.com

a wonderland of children's and young adult titles; several nooks hold comics, cookbooks, and inventory for a brisk online trade. The long entranceway displays Black-themed gifts and cards plus plenty of calendars of Vice President Kamala Harris, a daughter of Oakland. The center of the room delivers on what the weathered sandwich board outside promises passersby: "Books by and about Black people everywhere."

The Richardsons met at Tuskegee Institute and moved to San Francisco's Fillmore district a few years after graduation. In 1946, they opened Success Printing Co. and started publishing hard-to-find or out-of-print Black-authored books they'd collected during their travels. In 1960, as the Black Power movement was gaining prominence, they added bookselling and renamed their business Marcus Books. It became a hub of Black literary and political life. The store hosted forums and seminars on race and served as a meeting place for the Black Arts and Civil Rights movements. The Richardsons began providing books to incarcerated people across the country, which would become a long-standing commitment, and even put up their home as collateral to post bail for 100 students arrested during the 1968 protests at San Francisco State University, where Dr. Raye was the chair of the Black Studies Department for decades. Their daughter Blanche, who now co-owns

the business, says that her parents viewed books "as intertwined" with the long struggle for Black self-determination.

The Richardsons opened the Oakland location in 1976 (the publishing arm remained in San Francisco), and five years later, they moved the original S.F. shop into a purple Victorian at 1712 Fillmore Street. The historic building, the former site of Jimbo's Bop City, a staple in a neighborhood once known as the Harlem of the West for its vibrant Black businesses and huge jazz scene, housed Marcus Books downstairs and some of the family upstairs. A front patio hosted lively musical performances and readings until gentrification led to the Richardsons' losing the building in 2014. Despite a national outcry and a successful community fundraising campaign, they were unable to meet the new owners' asking price to buy back the property, and the family was forced to shutter the store.

Bookselling operations continued across the bay, however, and in 2020—a year of global pandemic *and* the Black Lives Matter movement—the store celebrated Marcus Books' 60th anniversary. At a time when just 6 percent of independent bookstores are Black-owned, Marcus Books preserves Bay Area literary history and serves as a beacon to bookstores around the nation. ∎

—**Faith Adiele**

The Booksmith

This indie offers readers an escape from the buzz of Haight Street.

I n 2011, *San Francisco Weekly* named the Booksmith the Best Re-imagined Bookstore. Christin Evans and Praveen Madan, the couple who'd bought the 31-year-old Haight-Ashbury business in 2007, had repainted the interior; expanded the graphic novel, magazine, and zine offerings; and launched a series of lively, literary game nights and other social events. Some of the best known included Shipwreck, which the Booksmith declared was "San Francisco's premier literary erotic fanfiction event" (it's unclear what, if any, were the other contenders); elaborate themed book launches; and BookSwap, wherein folks brought books on similar themes and were matched in discussion groups over cocktails before a big book swap at the end of the night.

In 2021, the Booksmith executed a second great reimagining. The shop moved one block down Haight Street into a performance space it was already leasing for events. Evans also co-owns the Alembic, a craft-cocktail bar next door that serves small bites, allowing attendees to nibble and sip during in-store events. The drinkery's slogan: "Read. Drink. Eat.

THE BOOKSMITH
1727 Haight St., San Francisco
booksmith.com

Think." Though the new location is about the same size as the previous one, it feels larger, with three rooms and multiple sections identified by colorful, hand-drawn and -lettered signs and by famous literary quotes on long, framed chalkboards. Luxe touches like Turkish rugs, end tables with potted plants, and a little reading alley appointed with tufted leather settees invite customers to settle in and read, which is just what Evans is hoping for. "Indies have to remain relevant," she says. "The chandeliers, the pop art magical eye, the shelf toppers with recommendations are all designed to create a good browsing experience, a space people want to spend time in."

The result is a refuge from Haight Street's craziness, a secret garden for booklovers seeking respite from psychedelic-colored Victorians, vintage-clothing shops, and hordes of tourists hoping to glimpse the Summer of Love.

The Booksmith's three rooms feature hand-drawn signs and thoughtful decor.

The Booksmith maintains strong community ties by hosting debut authors from the neighborhood for events and by using Upstream, a service pioneered by Daniel Handler, a.k.a. Lemony Snicket, that provides signed, personalized books for customers. The store also boasts strong offerings in rock biographies; art, fashion, and photography books; and cultural histories that honor the neighborhood's DNA. As befits an indie located in the birthplace of the 1960s counterculture movement, the Booksmith organized postcard-writing campaigns during the Trump administration, was one of the first stores to boycott Simon & Schuster for contracting controversial figure Milo Yiannopoulos, and is intentional about book buying that uplifts untold stories rather than promoting whatever New York is pushing. Even though independent bookstores make up only 10 percent of the U.S. book market, Evans explains, they're responsible for 50 percent of a book's first six months of sales: "Here at Booksmith, we take our role in connecting readers to new voices very seriously." ∎

—Faith Adiele

Anna Bullard, co-owner of Bookshop West Portal, "had always wanted to have a bookstore." She's witnessed many changes to the bookselling business throughout her time in the industry.

Bookshop West Portal

Lively events are the lifeblood of this neighborhood institution.

I've been a loyal customer of Bookshop West Portal for almost a decade. Located within walking distance of my home in San Francisco, this establishment is the ideal neighborhood bookseller, a place to be surrounded by books and booklovers. On a recent Independent Bookstore Day, the store bustled with activities. Adults played Bookstore Bingo, children drew the heroes of their favorite books, and tasty treats—donated by nearby restaurants—were served throughout the day. Nearby Fire Station 39 even dispatched a truck, several firefighters, and dozens of kid-size plastic helmets for fans of books like *Firefighter Frank* and *Firefighter Duckies!* All this and more took place as customers lined up at the registers and showed their support by buying books.

Founded in 2006, Bookshop West Portal is owned and operated by Anna Bullard and husband Neal Sofman, long-standing figures in the Bay Area book scene. "I had always wanted to have a bookstore," Bullard explains, adding that she became involved full-time at their store only a few years ago—which allowed Sofman to step back—though she's worked

BOOKSHOP WEST PORTAL
80 West Portal Ave., San Francisco
bookshopwestportal.com

in the industry for most of her adult life. Her experience includes bookstores in Chicago, a university press, and a Silicon Valley e-books company. Sofman, meanwhile, co-owned A Clean Well-Lighted Place for Books, a San Francisco literary institution that operated from 1982 to 2006.

Bullard and Sofman have seen it all, from the arrival of the big chains and the demise of many indies—there were a Waldenbooks and a used bookstore on the street when they opened Bookshop West Portal (both since closed)—to the rise of Amazon and the threat of e-books. "E-books completely—contrary to many, many people's predictions—really just completely leveled off. No one

really anticipated how the reading experience of the Kindle would actually not be that satisfactory for a lot of people," Bullard recalls, before adding, "Some people really love them." Then came the pandemic closures, which the shop weathered with online sales, home delivery, and help from nearby merchants. A hardware store and a mail-services outfit, which were deemed essential and permitted to remain open during lockdown, served as pickup points for book purchases.

With pandemic restrictions lifted, Bullard has been restoring the shop's full calendar of events and participating in neighborhood happenings like the West Portal Wine Walk, a Finding Waldo treasure hunt, and the Halloween Stroll. For in-store gatherings, wheeled shelves make way for rows of folding chairs beneath a ceiling adorned with colorful kites and a mobile of three whales, creating an intimate space for writers like Kim Stanley Robinson and Peggy Orenstein to be interviewed or to read from their latest works. Bullard is also planning for ticketed author events at nearby, larger venues. Before COVID-19, she organized this type of programming at the movie theater across the street, which has since shuttered—although a new owner may revive it. In the meantime, she is eyeing the gymnasium of a high school two blocks away. "Events are a big part of what we feel our mission is in terms of promoting authors and also just providing community service," Bullard says. She hopes that the store is known to all as "a welcoming community center." ■

—BLAISE ZEREGA

ALIBI BOOKSHOP
624 Marin St., Vallejo
alibibookshop.com

Within Vallejo's historic district, under an
awning of angled wooden shingles, stands
Alibi Bookshop. This literary beacon sponsors
a variety of in-store book clubs (including
one for young adults), coordinates to support
local arts events, and operates at the center
of an effort to revitalize the Vallejo business
community. Alibi maintains a lively Facebook page with frequent updates.

BANDUNG BOOKS
2289 International Blvd., Oakland
eastsideartsalliance.org/bandungbooks

Supported by Nomadic Press and the
EastSide Arts Alliance & Cultural Center in
Oakland, Bandung Books is a volunteer-run
space that offers a stunning collection of
new and used books by and about people of
color and houses archival materials of various
resistance movements, with plenty of places
to sit, read, and learn. Stop by any Thursday
at 8 p.m. for Holla Back!, Bandung's weekly poetry open mic night.

BOOK PASSAGE

51 Tamal Vista Blvd., Corte Madera
1 Ferry Building, San Francisco
bookpassage.com

For 47 years, readers, writers, and even
former U.S. presidents have made Book
Passage a North Bay literary destination. The
spacious layout of the Corte Madera shop
houses local, national, and international titles
as well as gift items, a café, and a meeting
area. With 800 annual author events and classes, like its Travel Writers &
Photographers and Mystery Writers Conferences, Book Passage may just be
"the Bay Area's liveliest bookstore."

BOOKS INC.

601 Van Ness Ave., San Francisco
3515 California St., San Francisco
2251 Chestnut St., San Francisco
1491 Shattuck Ave., Berkeley
1344 Park St., Alameda
2483 Washington Ave., San Leandro
74 Town & Country Village, Palo Alto
317 Castro St., Mountain View
1875 S. Bascom Ave., Ste. 600, Campbell
booksinc.net

In 1851, Bavarian immigrant Anton
Roman used his gold rush riches to fund a
bookselling-and-publishing venture. Despite
losing one location to the 1906 earthquake,
and no longer in the publishing game, Books
Inc. remains the West's oldest independent
bookseller, offering, from its nine locations,
community services like Alameda Queer
Teen Book Club at the shop on Park Street
and Bilingual Storytime at its Laurel Village
location on California Street.

BUILDERS BOOKSOURCE
1817 4th St., Berkeley
buildersbooksource.com

When it opened in 1982, Builders Booksource
was one of the first businesses on Berkeley's
Fourth Street. This chic store stocks books on
home building and landscaping, including
catalogs of up-to-date building code,
architecture volumes, and manuals for DIY
home projects. It also carries popular titles,
many by local authors; books on Bay Area hiking sites; and a children's
section curated by one of the owners, a school librarian.

CHRISTOPHER'S BOOKS
1400 18th St., San Francisco
christophersbooks.com

What's the secret to operating a hole-in-the-
wall bookstore in 2023? Careful curation, an
on-site owner, and a great landlord, according
to Tee Minot, who has run Christopher's since
1992. The shop dedicates a portion of its 650
square feet in sunny Potrero Hill to children's
and teen books, and the corner storefront has
made an appearance in an iconic San Francisco movie or two.

CITY LIGHTS BOOKSELLERS
& PUBLISHERS
261 Columbus Ave., San Francisco
citylights.com

Seventy years ago, poet Lawrence Ferlinghetti
cofounded City Lights Booksellers, the
nation's first all-paperback bookstore. Its
publishing arm brought Allen Ginsberg's
Howl and Other Poems to readers in 1956,
putting the Beats on the map. Locals and
pilgrims still flock to the landmark flat-iron building to nestle in the famous
poetry room and read rebellious works, both old and new.

THE COLLECTIVE OAKLAND
811 Broadway, Oakland
thecollectiveoakland.com

Anchoring a collective of Black businesses, this one-room bookshop offers a well-curated reading room with armchairs, Black art, and vintage vinyl. The tiny team that runs the Collective Oakland is taking Black literature to the people by launching book giveaways; creating partnerships with schools, hospitals, and farmers' markets; and hosting Read Drink Chill events with its in-house chef and mixologist.

COPPERFIELD'S BOOKS
138 N. Main St., Sebastopol
104 Matheson St., Healdsburg
1330 Lincoln Ave., Calistoga
775 Village Ct., Santa Rosa
140 Kentucky St., Petaluma
1300 1st St., Ste. 398, Napa
999 Grant Ave., Ste. 105, Novato
1200 4th St., San Rafael
2419 Larkspur Landing Circle, Larkspur
copperfieldsbooks.com

Inside the historic Analy Five & Dime building on Sebastopol's main street, you'll find a cozy, well-lit haven for exploring diverse titles displayed on wood shelves. This community hub hosts author events and serves as a hangout for locals who prize a good read and thoughtful recommendations from the book-loving staff. Copperfield's operates eight other locations in the North Bay.

EAST BAY BOOKSELLERS
5433 College Ave., Oakland
ebbooksellers.com

Formerly a location of Diesel, a Bookstore,
East Bay Booksellers is a hip staple of
Oakland's Rockridge neighborhood where you
can buy new books, planners, and stationery—
and have them gift wrapped. The store has a
large children's corner that feels like a secret
garden, plentiful staff picks arranged on
dedicated shelves, and magazines. It also supports the Prisoners Literature
Project, delivering books purchased by customers for incarcerated people.

FOREST BOOKS
1748 Buchanan St., San Francisco
forestbooks.org

In a quiet corner of Japantown, visitors will
feel immediately at peace among Forest
Books' stacks of used and rare collectible
titles. The store specializes in Zen philosophy,
so it's no surprise that owner Jakushu Gregory
Wood hosts a weekly meditation there on
Saturday mornings. "The forest awaits you.
Take your ease," reads a poem taped to one of the shelves.

GREEN APPLE BOOKS
506 Clement St., San Francisco
1231 9th Ave., San Francisco

From quirky in-store events and downloadable
Zoom backgrounds to a curated fiction
delivery service and Mergatroid, the apple-
and-book-toting mascot out front, this
legendary Clement Street store oozes whimsy.
Customers who wander Green Apple's maze
of new and used books will also find LPs, and
even the occasional couple getting engaged.

HICKLEBEE'S CHILDREN'S BOOKS
1378 Lincoln Ave., San Jose
hicklebees.com

Now entering its 44th year in business, Hicklebee's remains San Jose's most cherished children's bookstore, occupying a quaint spot on Willow Glen's main drag. Yet kids are not the only customers. Just to the right of the entrance, one finds an ample adult section with multiple genres. Ever supportive of the writer's trade, Hicklebee's allows any published author or illustrator to scribble on the walls, where room permits.

ISOTOPE: THE COMIC BOOK LOUNGE
326 Fell St., San Francisco
isotopecomics.com

In the comics-crazy Bay Area, Isotope stands out. The shop features pop art–style red-and-white leather couches and a display of illustrated toilet seats. Located in the Hayes Valley building where disco legend Sylvester used to throw his parties, Isotope offers new comics, graphic novels, hand-bound mini-comics, and events.

KEPLER'S BOOKS & MAGAZINES
1010 El Camino Real, Ste. 100, Menlo Park
keplers.com

Founded by peace activist Roy Kepler, this Silicon Valley bookstore was a gathering place for counterculture figures like Joan Baez and the Grateful Dead. Kepler's legacy as a leader of the paperback revolution of the 1950s and '60s has been kept alive with literary events and programs providing books for underserved local schools.

LEIGH'S FAVORITE BOOKS
121 S. Murphy Ave., Sunnyvale
leighsbooks.com

Located on historic Murphy Street in
downtown Sunnyvale, Leigh's Favorite Books
arranges hardcovers in a vividly eclectic
manner, with female and LGBTQ voices,
immigrant narratives, diaspora fiction,
and chart-toppers on prominent display.
Offering a 20 percent discount on hardcover
bestsellers and 50 percent on bestseller buybacks, Leigh's seeks to make book
buying affordable. Its companion shop next door, Bookasaurus, is a children's
book mecca.

MEDICINE FOR NIGHTMARES BOOKSTORE & GALLERY
3036 24th St., San Francisco
medicinefornightmares.com

In November 2021, a trio of City Lights, Dog
Eared Books, and Nomadic Press veterans
took over this storefront in the Mission
district to create a "Curative for Colonial
Nightmares." The light-filled bookshop and
gallery centers Black, Indigenous, and POC
voices and favors playful shelf tags like "The Kind of Musica Your Abuelita
Would Get Mad at You for Listening To."

MOE'S BOOKS
2476 Telegraph Ave., Berkeley
moesbooks.com

Beneath the distinctive red-and-white awning
and photos immortalizing legendary radical
and cofounder Moe Moskowitz, customers are
now greeted by daughter and current owner
Doris. Moe's Books, called "one of America's
very best" by the *New York Times*, offers
200,000 new and used titles, including rare
books in a room on the fourth floor.

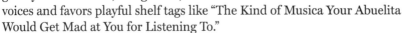

MORTI'S USED BOOK NOOK AND CAT ADOPTION LOUNGE
2200 Petaluma Blvd. N., Ste. 500, Petaluma
petalumapetpals.org/mortibooksandcats

Named for a kitten that founder Tanya Reyes says changed her life, Morti's has been home to adoptable cats since September 2021. It's supported by donations and weekend sales of low-priced used books like John Ash cookbooks and fiction by Amy Tan. The Facebook page chronicles heartwarming interactions.

MRS. DALLOWAY'S LITERARY AND GARDEN ARTS
2904 College Ave., Berkeley
mrsdalloways.com

Mrs. Dalloway's is a spacious bookstore in the Elmwood neighborhood, with two rooms and several nooks that serve as thematic display spaces for a large (and prominent) gardening section, art books, titles by Virginia Woolf (whose character Clarissa Dalloway inspired the store's name), and more.

OMNIVORE BOOKS ON FOOD
3885A Cesar Chavez St., San Francisco
omnivorebooks.myshopify.com

Omnivore Books feeds a Bay Area public obsessed with food. In the bright, cozy, culinary-themed space, owner Celia Sack stocks vintage, antiquarian, and modern titles on food and drink, including local and international voices. Chefs, home cooks, and foodies can enjoy a healthy menu of author events.

ORINDA BOOKS
276 Village Square, Orinda
orindabooks.com

A light and airy space with lots of room to
sit down and relax, Orinda Books makes
everyone feel welcome. Owner Pat Rudebusch
and his staff go the extra step to find the book
you need to read. You'll never visit without
engaging in a conversation, because Orinda
Books fosters connections—it's that place
"where everybody knows your name."

PEGASUS BOOKS
2349 Shattuck Ave., Berkeley
1855 Solano Ave., Berkeley
5560 College Ave., Oakland
pegasusbookstore.com

If browsing zines, new and used books,
records, cassettes, and CDs in a shop where
everyone wears a mask sounds good to you,
then make a beeline for Pegasus Books'
Shattuck Avenue location. Kids and young
adults won't be disappointed by the selection either. While there, shop for
reading-related gifts and thumb through unique greeting cards.

POINT REYES BOOKS
11315 Hwy. 1, Point Reyes Station
ptreyesbooks.com

Travel to West Marin means a hike, good food,
and a visit to Point Reyes Books. Stephen
Sparks and spouse Molly Parent, owners since
2017, honor the store's environmental legacy
while featuring poetry, fiction, and readings,
including virtual ones.

READERS' BOOKS
130 E. Napa St., Sonoma
readersbooks.com

Community loyalty counts at this 31-year-old bookshop. Cofounder Andy Weinberger's wine country gem highlights fiction, cookbooks, children's books, and readings by local authors like Ada Limón, its first employee at age 15. "Readers' Books will always feel like home to me," says Limón, now a National Book Critics Circle Award–winning poet.

RECYCLE BOOKSTORE
275 E. Campbell Ave., Campbell
1066 the Alameda, San Jose
recyclebookstore.com

This South Bay institution offers a vast inventory of used, rare, and out-of-print books. Its shops may be best known for their cats, however, who have their own page on the store's website and enthusiastic Instagram fans. Beloved feline Isbn, recognized by *Publishers Weekly* for Best Bookstore Cat Name, has relocated from Recycle's secondary branch in Campbell to the great bookstore in the sky.

RUSSIAN RIVER BOOKS & LETTERS
14045 Armstrong Woods Rd., Guerneville
booksletters.com

All bookstores have a personality, and Russian River Books has a warm one that greets you like an old friend. Owner Michael Rex is a teacher who cares about good books and his small-town community. He's created an inclusive place that offers free ESL night classes and letter-writing workshops.

SILVER SPROCKET
1018 Valencia St., San Francisco
silversprocket.net

This self-proclaimed "comic book store for
people who don't read comics" is a bright,
creative, inviting space for casual readers
and devoted makers alike. Silver Sprocket
sells books and zines from hundreds of
independent creators and presses (including
its own). You'll find classics of the genre like
Maus and *Persepolis* here, but you'll also discover handmade, self-published
comics from talented local artists.

SPACECAT
1415 W. San Carlos St., San Jose
superspacecat.com

Specializing in comics, graphic novels, video
games, and related ephemera, SpaceCat is a
popular collectors' shop tucked inside an old
building next to a midtown parking lot, where
it relocated about eight years ago. Rare *X-Men*
and *Avengers* comics line the walls above
stacks of brand-new books and magazines,
but for those who don't have time to browse, the store offers parking lot
pickups.

SPECTATOR BOOKS
4163 Piedmont Ave., Oakland
spectatorbooks.com

Even your dog is welcome at Spectator Books,
a store staffed by queer and nonbinary folks
committed to community. The shop is a
maze of new and used books for all ages.
It carries tarot cards and features curated
shelves of titles on local history, matters of
the occult, Black radicals, LGBTQ topics, and
psychedelics. Visit the website to learn about trading used books for store
credit.

TREEHORN BOOKS
625 4th St., Santa Rosa
treehorn.com

Only steps from Old Courthouse Square,
Treehorn Books is a mesmerizing place to
browse. It's run by cofounder Keith Hotaling
and his son, Grant, who was "born into
books." The extensive offerings include fiction,
children's books, titles by locals (Luther
Burbank, Gaye LeBaron, vintage Black
Sparrow Press editions), and works on art, philosophy, and World War II
history.

WORD HORDE EMPORIUM
OF THE WEIRD & FANTASTIC
2200 Petaluma Blvd. N., Ste. 805, Petaluma
weirdandfantastic.com

If you have a penchant for monster, horror,
and fantasy books, then Ross E. Lockhart's
shop of 3,500 curated independent and
small-press titles will be your favorite
destination. His lifelong fascination with the
genres was kindled when he was a young boy,
after watching the 1930s classic films *Frankenstein* and *King Kong*. ∎

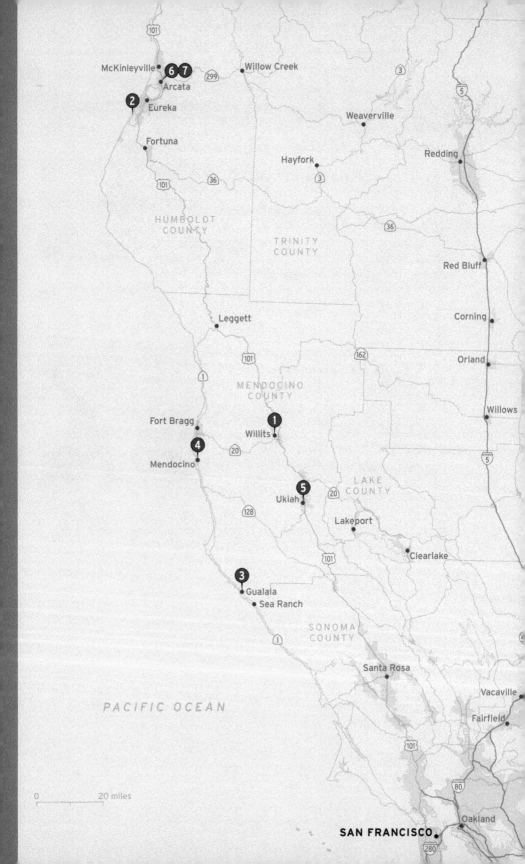

101

McKinleyville •
6 7
Arcata
299
Willow Creek

Weaverville

2
Eureka

Fortuna •

Redding •

Hayfork
3

HUMBOLDT
COUNTY

TRINITY
COUNTY

36

101
36
Red Bluff •

Corning •

Leggett •
162
Orland •

101
5

1
MENDOCINO
COUNTY
Willows •

Fort Bragg •
1
Willits
5

4
20
Mendocino •
LAKE
COUNTY

5
Ukiah •
20

128
Lakeport •

Clearlake •

101

3
Gualala •
Sea Ranch •

SONOMA
COUNTY

1
Santa Rosa •

Vacaville •

PACIFIC OCEAN
Fairfield •

101

0   20 miles

80

SAN FRANCISCO •
Oakland

280

BOOKSTORES | LEGEND

1 **THE BOOK JUGGLER**
182 S. Main St., Willits

2 **BOOKLEGGER**
402 2nd St., Eureka

3 **FOUR-EYED FROG BOOKS**
39138 Ocean Dr., Gualala

4 **GALLERY BOOKSHOP**
319 Kasten St., Ste. 270, Mendocino

5 **THE MENDOCINO BOOK COMPANY**
102 S. School St., Ukiah

6 **NORTHTOWN BOOKS**
957 H St., Arcata

7 **TIN CAN MAILMAN**
1000 H St., Arcata

NORTH COAST

Tin Can Mailman's name is inspired by its founder's time in the Peace Corps.

BOOKSTORE

TIN CAN
✳
MAILMAN
USED BOOKS

USED BOOKS

CLOSED

WATCH
YOUR
STEP

TIN CAN
✳
MAILMAN
USED BOOKS

NO SMOKING
NO VAPING

Tin Can Mailman

A former bank in Arcata now serves as a quiet reprieve from today's complicated world.

At lunchtime during my senior year at Arcata High School, I'd dart from class and hurry to my favorite bookstore, Tin Can Mailman. Once there, I had 22 minutes of undisturbed browsing through the store's labyrinth of shelves before I had to get back to school. I unearthed many secondhand paperbacks that I still have today: Sylvia Plath's *The Bell Jar*, Nathanael West's *The Day of the Locust*, and a stack of *Peanuts* comics, among them. Tin Can Mailman is the type of bookstore where you're left alone to follow your intellectual curiosity through a maze of dusty volumes—an experience not unlike reading itself.

Tin Can Mailman's building was erected in 1913, two blocks from the Arcata Plaza. It was originally a bank, which accounts for the store's unusual layout. The upper mezzanine, once offices, looks down onto the first-floor stacks. Shelves twist behind the children's room, which is in the former vault. Everywhere you look is packed with books.

TIN CAN MAILMAN
1000 H St., Arcata
tincanbooks.com

"We don't have a lot of floor space," says co-owner Margo Glenn-Lewis. "Pretty much every inch of that store that can have a bookshelf on it has a bookshelf on it."

Glenn-Lewis and her husband, Michael, purchased Tin Can Mailman in 2017. Recently retired, they saw the store come up for sale and drove up from Davis to take a look. Self-professed bookaholics, they fell in love and became the store's fourth owners.

Founder Will Mauck opened Tin Can Mailman in 1972. During his time in the Peace Corps, Mauck had visited the South Pacific archipelago Tonga, and he named the store after Niuafo'ou, or "Tin Can Island." The island had no

harbors for ships to dock in, so mail was stuffed into tin cans and thrown overboard for swimmers to retrieve. The store's brown-and-white wall hangings are a nod to the name—they're traditional Tongan tapa cloth.

Much to the relief of long-term customers, the new owners opted not to change much in the store. However, they did add a small selection of new books, mostly young adult and science fiction. The reason? Neil Gaiman.

"We couldn't keep Neil Gaiman books in stock," says Glenn-Lewis. "So I thought, We'll just buy the silly things new. And then we started taking special orders as well."

Despite this, Tin Can Mailman remains dedicated to used books, which is important in a college town, where half-price textbooks are a relief to students. (Nearby Cal Poly Humboldt was established the same year Tin Can Mailman's building was constructed.) Equally important is the inclusivity that comes with selling a large assortment of books. The store's motto is that it doesn't matter what you read, as long as you're reading.

As a result, Tin Can Mailman's bestsellers are as quirky as Humboldt County itself: Books on mushrooms are popular. So are sci-fi, children's books, new age, young adult, philosophy, and hiking guides.

After five decades, Tin Can Mailman continues to be a Humboldt staple. It offers a reprieve from this complex, fragmented world that's as simple as a search for a good book.

"It's really nice on a cold rainy day to go upstairs and park yourself in one of the bays near a window with a book," says Glenn-Lewis. "People have done that in the past. They'll come in with a bagel and a coffee and go upstairs. Then later we'll see them without the bagel and with an empty coffee cup, and a pleased look on their faces." ∎

—Joy Lanzendorfer

COOKBOOKS

COOK
BOOKS

The shop's co-owner
Margo Glenn-Lewis
(left) and store manager
Larissa Trageser create
an environment where
shoppers can browse to
their hearts' content.

THE BOOK JUGGLER
182 S. Main St., Willits
thebookjuggler.com

To learn how much Willits loves the Book
Juggler, read the online reviews: "Small
town jewel," "Marvelous," "Like stepping
into a powerful magical realm of universal
imagination." In addition to an abundance of
books, there are puzzles, games, DVDs, CDs,
records, and instruments. The store is staffed
by, in its words, "the friendliest weirdos on earth" and bookstore dog Zeus.

BOOKLEGGER
402 2nd St., Eureka
facebook.com/people/booklegger/100064419350168

Booklegger, in Eureka's Old Town, is a maze
of shelves where one can happily get lost.
With over 50,000 used and new books, the
store offers a diverse mix for every interest.
Want to read about aviation? Railroads?
Shakespeare? A foreign language? Booklegger
has a section for that.

FOUR-EYED FROG BOOKS
39138 Ocean Dr., Gualala
foureyedfrog.com

When Four-Eyed Frog Books was going
out of business, the community rallied
behind it. Nearly two dozen residents pooled
their money and created a co-op. This
heartwarming togetherness is represented by
the frog figurines throughout the space, which
is small but meets the needs of its community,
offering new releases, books by local authors, and a used section.

GALLERY BOOKSHOP
319 Kasten St., Ste. 270, Mendocino
gallerybookshop.com

Thanks to the carefully chosen selection at
Gallery Bookshop, intriguing books face
out from every shelf. While kids enjoy the
Bookwinkle's Children's Books room in the
back, adults can expand their comfort zone
inside this cheerful historic building. Great
Catsby, the resident kitty, often sits in the
window enjoying the view of the Pacific Ocean.

THE MENDOCINO BOOK COMPANY
102 S. School St., Ukiah
mendocinobookcompany.com

The Mendocino Book Company, in downtown
Ukiah, is a classic independent bookstore,
complete with a dignified awning out front.
This airy, well-lit room highlights a selection
of new releases on wooden tables, perfect for
finding the latest must-read. Since 1978, the
shop has resolutely turned attention away
from itself and back where it belongs: on the books.

NORTHTOWN BOOKS
957 H St., Arcata
northtownbooks.com

Northtown Books opened in 1965 and has
continually offered new releases, works by
local authors, and thought-provoking political
titles. In addition to a selection on Humboldt
County's redwood forests, there's a large
magazine section—a rare sight these days.
Each purchase comes with a free bookmark
designed by owner Dante DiGenova. ∎

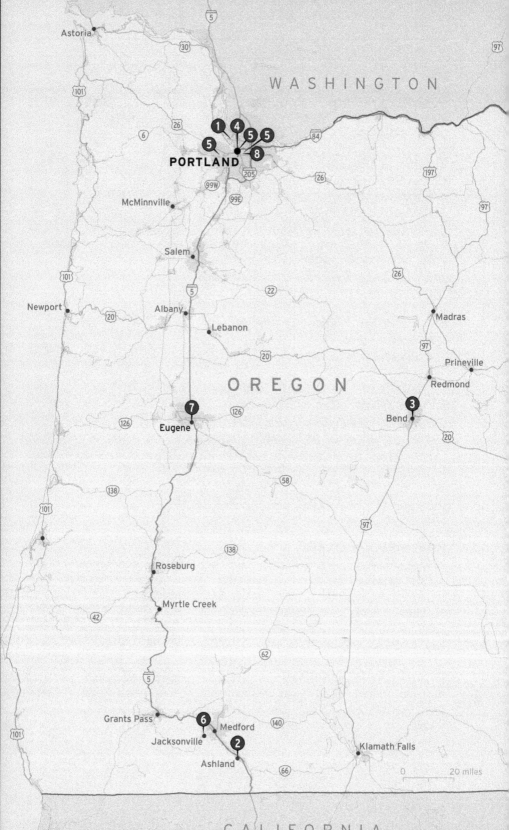

ASTORIA

WASHINGTON

PORTLAND

McMinnville

Salem

Newport

Albany

Lebanon

OREGON

Madras

Prineville

Redmond

Bend

Eugene

Roseburg

Myrtle Creek

Grants Pass

Jacksonville

Medford

Ashland

Klamath Falls

CALIFORNIA

0   20 miles

BOOKSTORES | LEGEND

1 ARCHES BOOKHOUSE
8900 N. Wall Ave., Portland

2 BLOOMSBURY BOOKS
290 E. Main St., Ashland

3 DUDLEY'S BOOKSHOP CAFE
135 NW Minnesota Ave., Bend

4 MOTHER FOUCAULT'S BOOKSHOP
523 SE Morrison St., Portland

5 POWELL'S BOOKS
1005 W. Burnside St., Portland
3723 SE Hawthorne Blvd., Portland
3415 SW Cedar Hills Blvd., Beaverton

6 REBEL HEART BOOKS
157 W. California St., Jacksonville

7 SMITH FAMILY BOOKSTORE
525 Willamette St., Eugene

8 THIRD EYE BOOKS ACCESSORIES & GIFTS
2518 SE 33rd Ave., Portland

OREGON

Craig Florence, owner of Mother Foucault's Bookshop, has created a cozy environment for conversation, contemplation, and thousands of books.

Mother Foucault's Bookshop

An old-world charm awaits those who enter this literary paradise.

As its name suggests, Mother Foucault's is not a typical bookshop. Or rather, it might've been a typical bookshop in, say, early-20th-century Paris. Thousands of used books weigh down teeming shelves, while hundreds more are stacked waist-high on tables, desks, upholstered chairs, the floor—everywhere. An upright piano stands in one corner, also burdened with heaps of books. The news program *Democracy Now!* plays quietly from a small vintage radio as Walt Curtis, the "unofficial poet laureate of Portland," rhapsodizes nonstop about poetry while sharing a bottle of red wine with the shop owner, Craig Florence, who will likely offer you a glass as well. Mother Foucault's, in other words, is a bibliophile's paradise.

Florence, who grew up in Portland, worked at Shakespeare and Company for a spell in the 1990s, and Mother Foucault's is in many respects a tribute to the iconic Left Bank bookstore and its storied past as a mecca for expat

MOTHER FOUCAULT'S BOOKSHOP
523 SE Morrison St., Portland
motherfoucaultsbookshop.com

writers. Only instead of encountering Ginsberg, Burroughs, and Baldwin, you'll find local literati holding court. Florence opened the Southeast Portland shop in 2010, in a former tattoo parlor, and soon expanded into the neighboring space, installing a rare-book room, a book-lined catwalk, and a small stage for author readings. Everything from the shelves to the molding to the banisters was built with reclaimed wood from a local nonprofit.

Though every category is represented, the shop skews toward literature, poetry, drama, philosophy, and criticism. Of note: Mother Foucault's shelves various languages side by side, so if you're looking for an Italian or German

translation of *For Whom the Bell Tolls*, you'll find it next to the English version. But don't reach for your phone to look up which edition to buy. Signs throughout the store warn shoppers that "the use of mobile phones is prohibited." The 46-year-old Florence is something of a Luddite. He doesn't use the internet, he doesn't own a smartphone, and the bookstore has only a limited web presence. Mother Foucault's is a community space—a place for conversation and contemplation. You won't see any laptops here. Don't even ask about the Wi-Fi.

In the pre-pandemic days, Mother Foucault's hosted readings and other events, with dozens of attendees crammed shoulder to shoulder, sipping from paper cups of wine or cans of cheap beer. Florence hopes to return to hosting events soon, but first he has to do something about the piles of books that have since accumulated on every conceivable surface. He is, he admits, "drowning in books." Visitors shouldn't expect a quick and easy shopping experience, but that's entirely the point. Mother Foucault's is a place to spend an entire afternoon, either browsing the shelves, digging through the random stacks of books, or just having a seat in a cozy chair, cracking open a well-loved paperback, and sharing a long conversation (and maybe a bottle) with a friend. ∎

—SANTI ELIJAH HOLLEY

ARCHES BOOKHOUSE
8900 N. Wall Ave., Portland
archesbookhouse.com

In a residential neighborhood in North
Portland, a small and beloved bookstore
recently changed ownership and its name, but
maintains a similar inventory of thousands
of used, rare, and antiquarian books.
Adam McInturf—a longtime bookseller
and store manager at the former Windows
Booksellers—took over ownership in 2022 and rebranded the shop as Arches
Bookhouse, which focuses on "across-the-board humanities."

BLOOMSBURY BOOKS
290 E. Main St., Ashland
bloomsburyashland.com

Bloomsbury Books takes its name from a
group of early-20th-century English writers
and thinkers that included, most notably
for this Ashland store, Virginia Woolf, who
serves as a sort of patron saint. Opened by
four women in 1980, the bright and cozy shop
carries a large selection of fiction, nonfiction,
and literary-themed gifts.

DUDLEY'S BOOKSHOP CAFE
135 NW Minnesota Ave., Bend
dudleysbookshopcafe.com

With its well-curated new and used titles,
including a collection of hiking books and
trail guides, and a first-floor coffee shop,
Dudley's already stands out in downtown
Bend. Add to those features the store's pine
floors, Douglas fir beams, and Dutch door,
and you've got what longtime owner Tom
Beans accurately calls an "eclectic, cozy" atmosphere.

POWELL'S BOOKS
1005 W. Burnside St., Portland
3723 SE Hawthorne Blvd., Portland
3415 SW Cedar Hills Blvd., Beaverton
powells.com

Powell's needs no introduction. Though a couple of smaller outposts exist in the Portland area, it's the flagship store on West Burnside, in the city's Pearl district, that is world-famous as the largest independent new and used bookstore on Earth, with multiple floors occupying a city block.

REBEL HEART BOOKS
157 W. California St., Jacksonville
rebelheartbooks.com

In a town with approximately 3,000 people, running a great bookstore isn't easy. Yet Rebel Heart celebrated its fifth anniversary by adhering to its maxim: "Be brave, be true, leave your mark." This small establishment (625 square feet) is located inside a historic former blacksmith's building, where a staff of three maintains the distinctive inventory.

SMITH FAMILY BOOKSTORE
525 Willamette St., Eugene
smithfamilybookstore.com

Opened in 1974 and since relocated to a historic building in Eugene's Market district, Smith Family Bookstore is a local institution. Carrying new and used books, the shop prides itself on offering a wide selection "for everybody, whether you're pursuing a PhD in philosophy or you just want to fix your bike," says owner Evon Smith.

THIRD EYE BOOKS ACCESSORIES & GIFTS
2518 SE 33rd Ave., Portland
thirdeyebag.com

Located in one of the whitest neighborhoods in the so-called whitest city in America, the Black-owned and -operated Third Eye Books provides a singular and essential service to Portland. Inside a small renovated house, you'll find titles by Black authors or on Black subjects, from radical histories to children's books to cookbooks. ■

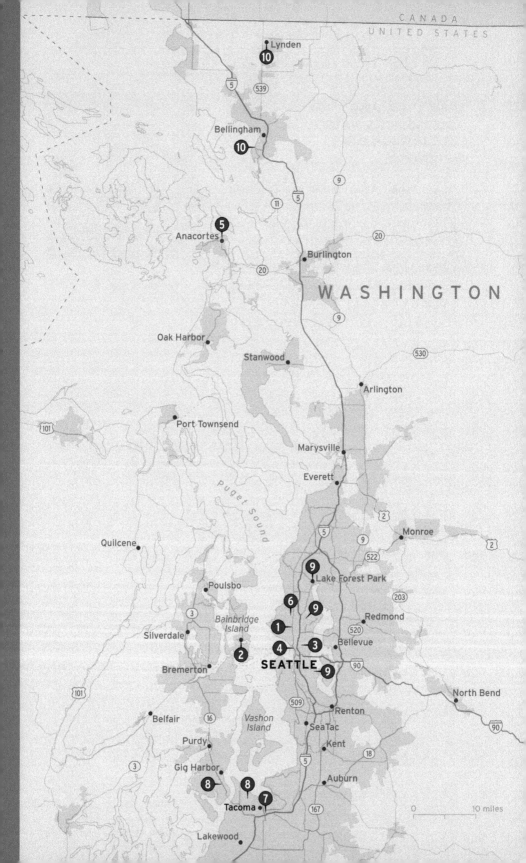

BOOKSTORES | LEGEND

1 BOOK LARDER
4252 Fremont Ave. N., Seattle

2 EAGLE HARBOR BOOK CO.
157 Winslow Way E., Bainbridge Island

3 ELLIOTT BAY BOOK COMPANY
1521 10th Ave., Seattle

4 LEFT BANK BOOKS
92 Pike St., Seattle

5 PELICAN BAY BOOKS & COFFEEHOUSE
520 Commercial Ave., Anacortes

6 PHINNEY BOOKS
7405 Greenwood Ave. N., Seattle

7 TACOMA BOOK CENTER
324 E. 26th St., Tacoma

8 TEACHING TOYS AND BOOKS
2624 N. Proctor St., Tacoma
4635 Point Fosdick Dr., Ste. 300, Gig Harbor

9 THIRD PLACE BOOKS
5041 Wilson Ave. S., Seattle
17171 Bothell Way NE, Ste. A101,
Lake Forest Park
6504 20th Ave. NE, Ravenna

10 VILLAGE BOOKS AND PAPER DREAMS
1200 11th St., Bellingham
430 Front St., Lynden

WASHINGTON

Left Bank Books is located near the entrance to Seattle's Pike Place Market. Its inventory, decor, and calendar of events reflect the shop's anarchist sensibilities.

Left Bank Books

A slice of antiestablishment culture thrives in a Big Tech haven.

It gets harder all the time to be eccentric in Seattle. The financial squeeze of living in a city ever more dominated by tech behemoths like Amazon and Microsoft means that truly alternative institutions can have a rough go of it. Left Bank Books proudly carries the torch. In a warren of rooms near the entrance to the Pike Place Market, Left Bank has operated as an anarchist collective for almost 50 years, and if you think that's easy, then you haven't ever (1) met any anarchists or (2) done anything collectively.

Left Bank's shelves are jammed with books of queer theory, labor history, Marxist and anarchist philosophy, and all the poetry you could ever want. For years, the front room—facing the madly busy market—was devoted to fiction, divided into books by male authors on one wall and female authors on the opposite one. Back in the 1970s, when the store opened, this was a bold feminist approach to bookselling. With its primo location, Left Bank attracts a huge amount of tourist traffic, and not too long ago the collective switched things up, moving more political books to the front so tourists would know exactly what they were getting themselves into from the moment they stepped in the door.

LEFT BANK BOOKS
92 Pike St., Seattle
leftbankbooks.com

In its endeavors and its very presence, Left Bank is a reminder that other ways of being and thinking exist outside the atmosphere of mindless consumption in which most of us reside. The collective has a publishing project that puts out an eclectic assortment of radical work. Left Bank also sponsors the Books to Prisoners program, which for half a century has put books into the hands of incarcerated folks.

It's just right that Left Bank is in the market, not simply because the market is the real soul of Seattle but also because so much of the city's labor history has taken place on the surrounding streets. In the early 20th century, the rabble-rousers of the Industrial Workers of the World—or Wobblies, as they were affectionately known—would climb onto soapboxes and declaim the rights of the worker on the very bricks that pave the street in front of Left Bank.

Full disclosure: I was a Left Bank volunteer when I was in high school, way back in the 1980s. I learned from my comrades about apartheid and Solidarnosc, gay pride (as we then called it) and Bakunin. A wild man used to swing by to talk our ears off every week or two, and this turned out to be the outlaw poet Steven Jesse Bernstein, who went on to open for Nirvana and Soundgarden, at least once with a live rodent hanging out of his mouth.

A couple of years ago, my son also volunteered at Left Bank—in this era, gender theory and Marxism were much under discussion. He met with a study group on Saturday evenings after the store closed. The front-room lights were turned off, and the group gathered in the bowels of the building to discuss the deeply impenetrable writings of the French philosopher Gilles Deleuze.

This story represents what I love about Left Bank and what I don't want lost from Seattle: this secret knowledge, this commitment to art, this profound weirdness, this disruption of the late-capitalist sheen that overlays our city. Left Bank is the Seattle I want to keep. ∎

—CLAIRE DEDERER

BOOK LARDER
4252 Fremont Ave. N., Seattle
booklarder.com

A mecca for cooks and readers alike, Book Larder has, for over 10 years, offered not just cookbooks but also classes and author events encompassing every kind of food and cuisine. Housed in a sunny storefront in the eternally funky Fremont neighborhood, the shop has a cheerful vibe that belies the extreme seriousness of the cooks who gather here.

EAGLE HARBOR BOOK CO.
157 Winslow Way E., Bainbridge Island
eagleharborbooks.com

Eagle Harbor is the center of activity on Bainbridge Island—supplying gifts for kids' birthday parties, supporting book groups, and hosting book launches for the island's multitude of well-known resident authors, including luminaries like David Guterson, Jonathan Evison, and Susan Wiggs. Eagle Harbor makes a great part of a day trip to Bainbridge, an easy and gorgeous 35-minute ferry ride from downtown Seattle.

ELLIOTT BAY BOOK COMPANY
1521 10th Ave., Seattle
elliottbaybook.com

The grande dame of Seattle booksellers, Elliott Bay anchors Capitol Hill's Pike-Pine corridor with a cathedral-like, wood-lined, two-story space in an old warehouse. For decades, led by book-industry darling Rick Simonson, Elliott Bay has been the place where writers dream of reading from their work and readers gather to support and sometimes revere them.

PELICAN BAY BOOKS & COFFEEHOUSE
520 Commercial Ave., Anacortes
pelicanbaybooks.com

Used bookstores come in all shapes and sizes, and, as with children, each one deserves our love. But there's something really special about a used bookstore that is jam-packed with books and yet remains open, light, and airy. Pelican Bay claims a street corner in maritime Anacortes and over the years has become a sunshiny hub of the main drag. Never have used books been shown to better advantage.

PHINNEY BOOKS
7405 Greenwood Ave. N., Seattle
phinneybooks.com

Almost a decade ago, Tom Nissley bought Phinney Ridge's bookshop with his *Jeopardy!* winnings and turned it into a small-but-mighty model neighborhood bookstore, choosing titles and creating gatherings that match his customers' interests. Nissley is a gifted writer, and Phinney Books' weekly email newsletter has become a must-read among booklovers all over the world.

TACOMA BOOK CENTER
324 E. 26th St., Tacoma
facebook.com/people/the-tacoma-book-center/100071134429808

Between its giant red building of winding, narrow aisles lined with tightly packed floor-to-ceiling shelves and a nearby warehouse dedicated to internet stock, Tacoma Book Center is home to half a million titles, including a plethora of technical manuals on a variety of subjects. Although most of these are destined for online sales, let the store know in advance and it'll have a selection ready for in-person browsing.

TEACHING TOYS AND BOOKS
2624 N. Proctor St., Tacoma
4635 Point Fosdick Dr., Ste. 300, Gig Harbor
teachingtoysandbooks.com

From cloth binding for infants to board books
for toddlers to fully fledged chapter titles
for young adults, Teaching Toys and Books
has you covered for all your kids' reading
needs—and their playing needs, too. It has
hundreds of toys for sale and a staff armed
with knowledge about how each one operates. The store's second location,
Teaching Toys, Too, is in Gig Harbor.

THIRD PLACE BOOKS
5041 Wilson Ave. S., Seattle
17171 Bothell Way NE, Ste. A101, Lake Forest Park
6504 20th Ave. NE, Ravenna
thirdplacebooks.com

Each branch of this wonderful retailer boasts
stock so lush that a reader is dizzied by choice.
The Wilson Avenue location in Seward Park is
the newest addition, and it's distinguished by
a kosher restaurant, a bar, and a diverse and
political community of readers and booksellers.

VILLAGE BOOKS AND PAPER DREAMS
1200 11th St., Bellingham
430 Front St., Lynden
villagebooks.com

A three-story brick labyrinth in Bellingham's
historic Fairhaven neighborhood, Village
Books and Paper Dreams is built for aimless
wanderings and hyper-specific treasure hunts
alike. Just blocks from the waterfront, it's cozy
and sea-breezy, and while you need no excuse
to meander its aisles of books, maps, art, and Pacific Northwest history, most
find a literary gem to take home. For even more options, check out the store's
second location in nearby Lynden. ∎

BOOKSTORES | LEGEND

1 ARIZONA: CHANGING HANDS BOOKSTORE
6428 S. McClintock Dr., Tempe
300 W. Camelback Rd., Phoenix

2 ARIZONA: THE POISONED PEN BOOKSTORE
4014 N. Goldwater Blvd., Ste. 101, Scottsdale

3 IDAHO: REDISCOVERED BOOKS
180 N. 8th St., Boise
1310 W. State St., Boise
802 Arthur St., Caldwell

4 NEVADA: COPPER CAT BOOKS
1570 W. Horizon Ridge Pkwy., Ste. 170, Henderson

5 NEVADA: SUNDANCE BOOKS AND MUSIC
121 California Ave., Reno

6 NEVADA: THE WRITER'S BLOCK
519 S. 6th St., Ste. 100, Las Vegas

7 NEW MEXICO: COLLECTED WORKS BOOKSTORE & COFFEEHOUSE
202 Galisteo St., Santa Fe

8 NEW MEXICO: GARCIA STREET BOOKS
376 Garcia St., Santa Fe

9 NEW MEXICO: OP.CIT. BOOKS
157 Paseo de Peralta, Santa Fe
124A Bent St., Taos

10 UTAH: BACK OF BEYOND BOOKS
83 N. Main St., Moab

11 UTAH: UNDER THE UMBRELLA
511 W. 200 S., Ste. 120, Salt Lake City

OTHER NOTABLES

"People love a bookstore with personality," says Drew Cohen, who co-owns the Writer's Block with his husband, Scott Seeley. The pair has cultivated a lively literary community in the middle of Sin City.

The Writer's Block

Readers get their thrills at this literary underbelly of Las Vegas.

A stranded brainy tourist." That's Drew Cohen's unexpected answer to a question about the archetypal customer of the Writer's Block, the independent bookstore he co-owns in downtown Las Vegas. One might've anticipated a taxonomy of local book nerds, but really this makes just as much sense. Not all of the millions of annual visitors are here for a Sin City bender. Some are nongambling conventioneers or people visiting retired parents, and they're looking for a different indulgence. "It's something that's probably unique to us, somewhat unique in the country," Cohen says.

He does offer a partial taxonomy of local book nerds who patronize his store: downtown hipsters, young families, students and faculty from the University of Nevada, Las Vegas, kids from the nearby performing arts school, emissaries from deepest suburbia. What locals and out-of-towners share is, first, a profound relief at finding a refuge of literary culture in a city better known for its endless distractions. And second? Good taste.

"I didn't expect Las Vegas to be as literary-minded and highbrow as it is," says Cohen, who runs the store with his husband, Scott Seeley.

THE WRITER'S BLOCK
519 S. 6th St., Ste. 100,
Las Vegas, Nevada
thewritersblock.org

Not long after they opened (in a different location) in 2014, Cohen saw that his bestselling book was Albert Camus's *The Myth of Sisyphus*. It was an early sign that he wouldn't need to bait the shelves with mainstream fare to keep the doors open.

Success was by no means ensured—most previous attempts to establish a truly independent bookstore in Las Vegas had foundered; the city wasn't ready. Cohen recalls hearing a few "dire predictions of failure" prior to opening. But years of steady population growth seem at last to have deposited enough high-end readers to sustain such an eclectic place. "We consistently sell esoteric fiction and super-new stuff," he says. "I think our selection can stand shoulder to shoulder with bookstores in New York or Seattle."

Along with its vanguard and small-press fiction, the store's 20,000-book inventory includes robust sections devoted to essays and memoirs, history, and poetry. It's all nestled in a visually arresting space that eschews the standard

Vegas mood board in favor of a sophisticated whimsy. This is thanks largely to Seeley, who brought his previous experience with the McSweeney's retail arm to bear—ersatz birds fill the rafters; quirky toys, games, and puzzles are everywhere; and in a witty twist on the bookstore cat, the Writer's Block has a beloved bunny named the Baron.

This makes canny business sense—"People love a bookstore with personality," Cohen says—but it has also made the Writer's Block a hub for a literary community that hasn't always had one. Local writers hang around, jockeying their laptops in the coffee shop, chatting up the young, bookish staff. There are reading groups—a toast to the Bourbon Book Club!—and free writing workshops for kids.

"In many ways, the Writer's Block is literary church," emails Kim Foster, a James Beard Award–winning writer and frequent habitué of the store. "On any given night you can hear literary giants like Leslie Jamison and Claire Vaye Watkins read their work there, next to a young Mexican poet doing his first reading, or watch a formerly incarcerated Egyptian activist read his work after seeking literary asylum in Vegas."

"Even if I just lived in Las Vegas and had another job," Cohen says, "I would probably hang out at our store." ■

—SCOTT DICKENSHEETS

ARIZONA: CHANGING HANDS BOOKSTORE

6428 S. McClintock Dr., Tempe
300 W. Camelback Rd., Phoenix
changinghands.com

Changing Hands Bookstore has been a haven for Tempe, Arizona, booklovers since 1974. The independent store, located in a typical southwestern-style shopping center, sells new and used books and hosts hundreds of author events annually. Its second location, which includes the First Draft Book Bar, opened in a historic redbrick building in central Phoenix in 2014 and offers beer, wine, coffee, and, yes, more books.

ARIZONA: THE POISONED PEN BOOKSTORE

4014 N. Goldwater Blvd., Ste. 101, Scottsdale
poisonedpen.com

Behind the walls of a modest storefront in Old Town Scottsdale lurk murder, mayhem, and mystery. Fortunately, all this violence lies between the covers on the Poisoned Pen's shelves. The longtime independent, which also offers historical fiction, science fiction, and Southwest-centric titles, hosts events both in-house and virtually.

IDAHO: REDISCOVERED BOOKS

180 N. 8th St., Boise
1310 W. State St., Boise
802 Arthur St., Caldwell
rdbooks.org

To create "a place where books and people meet," Boise's downtown literary hub hosts more than 200 book events for adults and kids annually. This year, Rediscovered Books aims to give away 1,500 titles through the Read Freely Project, which provides 10 free copies of a featured book to individuals, to be distributed to whomever they choose. The only stipulation: the books must be handed out face-to-face.

NEVADA: **COPPER CAT BOOKS**
1570 W. Horizon Ridge Pkwy., Ste. 170, Henderson
coppercatbooks.com

You can see why this is among the few used bookshops left in the Las Vegas area. The selection is well organized and all over the map—from UFO studies to plump history shelves to *Trump: Divine Intervention or Not?* But it goes deep in surprising spots—so much Nabokov!—and, importantly, the inventory changes often. Only disappointment? Mickey, the bookstore cat, is black, not copper.

NEVADA: **SUNDANCE BOOKS AND MUSIC**
121 California Ave., Reno
sundancebookstore.com

Sundance calls itself "a creative tavern of the soul"—and backs it up. The wow factor of its colonnaded exterior—it occupies a century-old mansion—is matched inside by two floors of books anchored by a robust section of Nevada-oriented titles. Its alcoves and chairs encourage dawdling and conversation, and it even operates a publishing imprint.

NEW MEXICO: **COLLECTED WORKS BOOKSTORE & COFFEEHOUSE**
202 Galisteo St., Santa Fe
collectedworksbookstore.com

Founded in 1978, Collected Works is the oldest of Santa Fe's 18 independent bookstores. Inside you'll find a coffee shop, a fireplace, a patio, puzzle and chess tables, resident terrier Elizabeth Barrett Brownie, and multiple places to sit and browse any of the store's 25,000 volumes (emphasis on southwestern literature, history, and cooking). Readings, book signings, and discussions occur regularly.

NEW MEXICO: GARCIA STREET BOOKS
376 Garcia St., Santa Fe
garciastreetbooks.com

Over 30 years in business, this cozy eastside shop has focused on community connection. Staff will happily place special orders, offer curbside pickup, and provide home delivery. Discount tables guard the portal leading to an eclectic selection of fiction, nonfiction, and children's books plus cards and book-themed merchandise.

NEW MEXICO: OP.CIT. BOOKS
157 Paseo de Peralta, Santa Fe
124A Bent St., Taos
opcit.com

Op.Cit. is a bookhunter's dream: 30,000-plus volumes—mostly used, some new—stacked and shelved in the flagship Santa Fe store (the Taos location is smaller and tidier). Prices range from free to over a thousand dollars for collectible titles. Author events are starting up again post-pandemic, and the Taos Op.Cit. hosts a monthly mystery book club.

UTAH: BACK OF BEYOND BOOKS
83 N. Main St., Moab
backofbeyondbooks.com

Owned by a former volunteer national park ranger, the premier bookstore in Utah's red-rock canyon country is stocked with guidebooks, Native histories, environmental literature, and works by southwestern writers like Tony Hillerman, Barbara Kingsolver, and Edward Abbey. The name comes from Abbey's classic novel of eco-sabotage *The Monkey Wrench Gang*, but it suits the entire region.

UTAH: **UNDER THE UMBRELLA**
511 W. 200 S., Ste. 120, Salt Lake City
undertheumbrellabookstore.com

More than two dozen volunteers keep the wheels of Under the Umbrella turning. The store sells only titles by or about queer people and features a "give and take" wall, stocked with gift cards, concert tickets, prepurchased books, and more; contraceptives in the bathrooms; and meeting spaces that can be reserved for events. ■

INDEX

W

CONTRIBUTORS

WRITERS
Faith Adiele
Jessica Blough
Sara Borjas
Lee Bruno
Elizabeth Casillas
Jane Ciabattari
Kim Cross
Marcus Crowder
Claire Dederer
Scott Dickensheets
Samantha Dunn
Andrea A. Firth
Nasim Ghasemiyeh
Michelle Cruz Gonzales
M.T. Hartnell
Santi Elijah Holley
Robert Ito
Michael Jaime-Becerra
Kade Krichko
Joy Lanzendorfer
Ken Layne
Jaya Padmanabhan
Anne Pedersen
Gary Singh
Julian Smith
David L. Ulin
Mark Wallace
Amy E. Wallen
Paul Wilner
Blaise Zerega

PHOTOGRAPHERS
Joe Buglewicz
David Calvert
Mike Kai Chen
Christina Gandolfo
Penni Gladstone
Amy Kumler
John Lok
Charlie Neuman
Celeste Noche
Tod Seelie
Max Whittaker

Photographs included in the listings sections are courtesy of the bookstores' social media accounts.

CARTOGRAPHER
Matt Twombly

Is your favorite indie bookstore missing from this guide? Drop us a line at bookstores@altaonline.com to let us know whom we missed and why they should be included. Visit altaonline.com/bookstores for frequent additions.

Join *Alta.*

Show Your Love for California and the West

Alta Journal members share a passion for California and the West—and we're committed to deepening that feeling with award-winning journalism, fiction, and poetry, along with a vibrant community.

LEARN MORE AT ALTAONLINE.COM/JOIN